D1188589

MODERN GLOOM AND CHRISTIAN HOPE

HILDA GRAEF

Modern Gloom and Christian Hope

HENRY REGNERY COMPANY • 1959

Nihil Obstat:
　　　RICHARD ROCHE, D.D.
　　　　　Censor Deputatus

Imprimatur:
　　✠ FRANCIS J. GRIMSHAW, D.D.
　　　　Archiepiscopus Birmingamiensis
　　　　10 March 1959

© HENRY REGNERY COMPANY
64 E. Jackson Blvd.
Chicago 4, Illinois

Manufactured in the United States of America
Library of Congress Catalog Card Number 59-10546

Contents

Preface

THE present brief study of modern thought and literature is intended solely as a criticism of contemporary
pessimism from the Christian point of view. For many
years the author has been struck by the tremendous
success of just those writers who consistently portray the
dark sides of life and stress the meaninglessness of "existence," an attitude which has also made considerable
inroads on quite a few professedly Christian and Catholic thinkers, dramatists and novelists. It is the purpose
of this book briefly to analyze the works of some representatives of this thought and to show its opposition to
an authentic Christian outlook, with its emphasis on
hope and its rejection of "dread" and despair, the pet
subjects of so much recent writing. But this criticism of
the contemporary literary scene from the Catholic point
of view implies no literary judgments. Several of the
authors discussed in this study are excellent writers—
but the artistic merit of their work does not enter into
this discussion. Our point of view is solely that of the
Christian, for whom hope is one of the theological virtues and despair a sin, and the writers treated in this
book are viewed almost exclusively from this angle.

So as to make this study accessible to a wider public
the choice of subjects had to be severely limited, and we

have deliberately confined ourselves to some of the authors most widely known and read on both sides of the Atlantic, or at least, as in the case of Kierkegaard and Heidegger, of far-reaching influence on the modern mind. If our criticisms may seem in some cases unduly severe or far from hitting the mark, we would remind the reader that a balanced judgment of one's contemporaries is not easily achieved and that the following pages were prompted by the desire to show that a more positive view of human life than is fashionable at the moment is possible and, indeed, desirable even in this atomic age.

HILDA GRAEF

Oxford,
All Saints, 1958

MODERN GLOOM AND
CHRISTIAN HOPE

1

PESSIMISM FROM KIERKEGAARD TO ANOUILH

Søren Kierkegaard

It all began when, in October, 1841, a brilliant young graduate of Copenhagen University broke off his engagement to a charming young girl ten years his junior. Until then the young man had published a few not very important essays. But the broken-off engagement soon became a festering wound in his highly-strung nervous mentality. It was aggravated by the very peculiar education he had received from his sombre father, who professed a personal brand of self-torturing Lutheranism; and so the young Søren Kierkegaard found only one outlet for his emotional difficulties, and that was writing. This was the birth hour of existentialism, this peculiar, many-colored modern philosophy which has entered so many spheres of our life that one can hardly open a book on any serious subject (except science) without meeting the word "existential" at least once on every five or six pages.

Now the strange thing is that, though we bandy about

1

this term in season and even more out of season, people are hard put to it when asked to explain exactly what it means. I remember well a Protestant German theological periodical before the Second World War sending around a questionnaire asking fifty authorities to define what they meant by existentialism. These fifty learned men actually sent in fifty different answers; and even a philosopher like Father Copleston in his extraordinarily lucid book on Contemporary Philosophy has difficulties in finding a common denominator fitting such different persons as Kierkegaard, the German philosopher Heidegger, the French thinker and playwright Sartre, and a good many other representatives of this movement. One feature, however, they all have in common: they all have very little use for human reason, and consequently their view of man's life, or rather of "existence" to use their preferred technical term, is pessimistic. I say "consequently," because—for good or ill—man is a rational being, and if we take away his reason and deprive him of a rational view of things, there is not very much left to be proud of. This, as a matter of fact, was the reason why Pope Pius XII condemned existentialism in his Encyclical *Humani Generis* (August 12, 1950) "whether it denies God's existence or merely the validity of metaphysical reasoning."

Now we might simply say: if the Pope has condemned existentialism that's good enough for us—why should we worry about it any longer and concern ourselves with a movement that is so palpably wrong and dangerous to our faith? But this is precisely the reason why we must concern ourselves with it. For we live no longer in the Middle Ages, when it was sufficient for the Church to

condemn a movement and nothing more was heard of it—
at least openly, for often enough the heretical movements
would go underground and continue their destructive
work in secret. Today, however, this is no longer the case.
Existentialism and the pessimism it entails continues to
flourish, not only among the philosophers but on the
stage, in the cinema, in television, diffused more or less
explicitly and only too often implicitly through all the
media at our disposal, which are so infinitely more varied
and efficacious than those known to our fathers.

Now if we would understand a movement we must
begin at its source, and this is why this chapter starts
with the broken-off engagement of Kierkegaard, the father of existentialism. I have no intention to denigrate
this great influential thinker, who grappled with the problems of his life to the best of his ability and who was
himself a very unhappy man living in a world that did
not understand his problems. His breaking-off of his
engagement to Regine Olsen, whom he loved and who
loved him, was the act of a man at war with himself, a
neurotic unable to shoulder the responsibilities of married
life. Neither Regine nor Copenhagen society could understand his reasons; and he himself had to analyze the
whole situation in endless psychological discussions in
order to rid himself of the feeling of guilt and of his own
emotional unhappiness as well as he could. It is to this
personal event in his life that we owe the treatises that
have stirred so many contemporary authors: *Either-Or,
Fear and Trembling, Philosophical Fragments, The Concept of Dread, Stages on Life's Way,* and the various
Edifying Discourses. If we would rightly understand his

philosophy we must never forget its origin; for it was not conceived sitting back in a professorial chair, thinking serenely about the great questions of divine and human being, nature and spirit, right and wrong, as philosophers from Plato and Aristotle to Descartes and Hegel had done before him, but it was worked out to solve a quite personal problem: how can I, this miserable human individual Søren Kierkegaard, best grapple with the painful situation in which I find myself. In fact, his state of mind was not so very different from that of a certain monk, who, some 330 years before him, had tortured himself with the question: "How can I, Martin Luther, find a gracious God?" Both Luther's neurotic scrupulosity and Kierkegaard's inability to face the demands of normal human life led them to formluate, the one a novel theology, the other a novel philosophy. Theirs were indeed hard cases; but then hard cases not only make, as the saying goes, bad laws, they also make bad theology and bad philosophy. To consider the great metaphysical questions a man needs a calm, dispassionate mind. A deeply wounded human individual quivering with emotion is not really fit for such an intellectual pursuit, though, and this no doubt accounts partly for the success of this kind of philosophy; it is more interesting to read the violent outpourings of a tormented spirit than the objective expositions of a quiet mind. Besides, the former require much less sustained thought, whereas the latter have to be closely studied. Try to read an article from St. Thomas's *Summa Theologica* and you will find yourself poring over it and consulting commentaries; read a page or two from Kierkegaard's *Either-Or* and you will sail along without too much difficulty, borne away on the waves of the author's emotions.

For let us make no mistake, Kierkegaard's thought is emotional. In fact he reacts violently against the thought of the professional philosophers, which, according to him, has no relation to real life, to the "individual," which plays such an important part in Kierkegaard's teaching. Here again, we cannot condemn him, for it was his misfortune to have lived at a time and in surroundings where only one type of professional philosophy held sway—and that was Hegel's.

Now Hegel was one of the most influential, and at the same time one of the most pernicious thinkers Germany has produced, for he is the intellectual father of both Nazism and Marxism. His teaching is centred in a complete suppression of the individual and the exaltation of the impersonal "Spirit," incarnate in the various stages of human history, that sweeps along in the grand movement of thesis, antithesis and synthesis. In this movement evil is a necessary stage, whereas the individual human being is completely submerged, having no rights against, for example, the state, in which the spirit is at that moment incarnate. And in Hegel's time and in his opinion, this state was Prussia. The divine Trinity Itself was thus dissolved into an historical process, Father, Son and Holy Spirit corresponding to the Hegelian triad of thesis, antithesis and synthesis.

Since this was practically the only philosophy Kierkegaard was taught, it is not so surprising that he should have rebelled against it—both as a Christian and as an individual. But, as he was untrained in the old Christian tradition and in a state of emotional upheaval, it is not surprising either that he should have thrown out the baby with the bathwater. Man was not just a cog in the machine of the state but an individual, and nothing but an individual; his existence does not flow along within the historical process of thesis, antithesis and synthesis, but is always and everywhere determined by choice; God is not to be identified with the historical process but is totally different from man the "absolute paradox" and can be reached only by a "leap." If man is not to be simply one of many, if he is to "exist," he must choose himself in fear and anguish.

These are some of the crucial points of Kierkegaard's thought, and we must develop them a little further to understand how they came to have such a far-reaching influence on contemporary authors. First of all, by dissociating man entirely from his fellows, from life in community, Kierkegaard disregarded completely Aristotle's definition of man as a "political animal." Now it is true, man is by no means *only* that, but he is *also* that. This truth was expressed by Christ Himself, when He taught that we must give to God the things that are God's, but also to Caesar the things that are Caesar's. Nor is this all. Kierkegaard once said he wanted written on his tombstone: "That Individual." For him religion, too, was a wholly individualistic affair. Man stands before God alone. In his view man passes through three stages, which he calls the aesthetical, the ethical, and the religious. They are not consecutive, but so sharply divorced from each other that the second and the third can be reached only by a "leap."

In the first, aesthetical stage, man's main concern is with pleasure—not necessarily sensual pleasure; but his principal interest is to procure the greatest enjoyment from life. Now this leaves a taste of bitterness, for no enjoyment ever comes up to a man's expectations: "Marry," writes Kierkegaard in *Either-Or*, "you will regret it; don't marry, you will also regret it. Marry or do not marry, you will regret both. . . . Laugh at the stupidity of the world, you will regret it; weep over it, you will also regret it; whether you laugh or weep at the stupidity of the world, you will regret both. . . . Hang yourself, you will regret it; do not hang yourself, you will also regret it; hang yourself or don't hang yourself, you will regret both. . . . This, gentlemen, is the essence of all wisdom." The end of this "aesthetic" life is utter boredom, *ennui* as the French call it, ending in the cry of despair: "What can save me from the curse of this boredom?"

This is where the "leap" comes in. When a man has reached this total disgust with the "aesthetic" life, he is confronted with a choice: he must consciously "choose himself" as a being with a purpose, by an "absolute choice"—a leap into another, the ethical sphere. In this sphere he submits himself to the rule of the moral law, he lives with moral responsibility. Now this life makes man aware of something else in him, which also appears by a "leap," and this is sin. In the *Concept of Dread*, Kierkegaard gives a penetrating analysis of sin which, in his view, comes into being through "dread." Dread is not really a very good translation of the Danish word *Angest*, German *Angst*, which has overtones that cannot be quite adequately expressed by any English term, and which is one of the key words of all existentialist thought, whether religious or atheistic. For *Angst,* as distinct from fear, is something irrational: fear will always be aroused by some real or imagined cause; it is reasonable that we should be afraid of illness, poverty, death, and other calamities that may befall us. Existential *Angst,* on the other hand, is a psychological state requiring no external misfortune; it is, on the contrary, the woof and warp of human existence itself, because it is caused by man's freedom. When the spirit which, in the state of innocence, had been in a dreamlike condition, longs to awake, to exercise its freedom and to choose, it becomes giddy, as a man might become physically giddy when he stands on the brink of an abyss. This is man's state when his choice of a moral existence has acquainted him with sin. On the brink of despair, in the grip of dread, he has to make the final choice, for or against God. Kierkegaard has no use whatever for rational proofs of God's existence; God and reason are quite incompatible, because God is the absolute transcendent, which can be reached only by the "leap" of faith by which we "choose" Him. Hence God is accessible only to a personal decision of the individual, there is no objective certainty—indeed, in Kierkegaard's view, "truth is subjectivity."

This is why Kierkegaard makes so much use of the "paradox." For him Christianity is the "absolute paradox." For if God is absolutely transcendent, if there is no connection between Him and man, then the dogma that He became man in Christ is, indeed, utterly incomprehensible; it is the absolute paradox which can be held only by a faith that defies reason. This complete discontinuity gives Kierkegaard's thought a certain violence; he himself often uses the word "passionate," as if he were again and again trying to convince himself that he really does believe what he wants to believe. There is one significant saying which would seem to prove this: "I want integrity. If what this generation and my contemporaries want is this, if they want sincerely, honestly, without reserve, openly and outright to rebel against Christianity, to say to God, we can, we will not submit to this power, only let it be noted, if this is done sincerely, honestly, without reserve, openly and outright—then, however strange it may appear, I will join with them. For it is integrity I want."[1]

This shows clearly that, however sincere Kierkegaard's personal faith may have been, it rested on a very insecure foundation. If faith in God springs from dread and despair and is achieved only by a "leap" into the sphere of the absolute paradox, then, if the leap is made in another direction, it may just as well take a man into the sphere of atheism, as it actually did in the case of so many modern existentialists.

Martin Heidegger

Though Kierkegaard died in 1855 and his teaching had caused a considerable stir among his contemporaries in

---

[1] Cited in E. L. Allen, *Kierkegaard: His Life and Thought*, 1935, p. 110.

his native Denmark, his influence remained dormant for almost three quarters of a century, suddenly to leap into the limelight in the period between the two World Wars. This is not surprising: the prosperous nineteenth century with its faith in human progress had no use for a philosophy in which dread and despair played such an essential part. But it was admirably suited to the world of the twentieth, rent by total war and shaken to its foundations by dictatorships outstripping any cruelties that could be found in the pages of history books. The teaching of Kierkegaard was to bear fruit in Heidegger and Sartre, Anouilh and Camus.

There is, however, one great difference between Kierkegaard and these latter exponents of his principles. Kierkegaard lived his own teaching; his life ended in failure and bitterness. Our contemporary existentialists are highly successful philosophy professors and playwrights, who preach pessimism with a vengeance, but who seem themselves to be getting a remarkably large slice out of "existence." Where life and teaching show a too flagrant inconsistency, there is normally something wrong with either the one or the other. We will therefore cast a quick glance at what these authors have to say and examine whether it can really help a man to cope with life, which is what the existentialists are aiming at.

In 1933 Martin Heidegger, who had been brought up a Catholic and once wanted to be a Jesuit, became rector of Freiburg University. In his inaugural lecture he fulsomely welcomed the new age, Hitler's Third Reich, and, since such orations are most suitably adorned with some classical citations, he quoted Plato to the effect that all great things are in tempest. He was a wholehearted supporter of Nazism, this mass movement which catered to the lowest instincts of the German people and drove millions of Jews, "non-Aryan" Christians, Poles, and other "sub-human" creatures into the gas chambers—though he himself had studied philosophy under a Jew, Edmund Husserl. Nevertheless, Heidegger is still one of the most influential thinkers of our time.

His thought is somewhat difficult to understand, since he uses a peculiar terminology of his own, not found in any other system of thought. But for the purposes of this book it will suffice to outline just a few of his main ideas, and perhaps, stripped of their obscure linguistic attire, it will be found that they are not quite as profound as they seem. Heidegger begins with the undeniable fact that man is in the world, busy with the things that surround him. In this state he becomes a prey to the multiplicity of impressions and occupations and loses sight of the whole. He delivers himself to the anonymous crowd and surrenders the responsibility for his own existence— a description which seems to fit pretty accurately the state of mind of the followers of Hitler, whether philosophy professors or lesser fry. In any case, as a thinker at least Heidegger repudiates this attitude of the "mass mind," against which the voice of conscience revolts, calling a man to *Eigentlichkeit*, which means something like actuality or reality. If a man leaves the "being in the mass," which Heidegger calls "inauthentic existence," he will experience himself as "thrown into the world," a finite being destined to death, and this "thrown-ness" is experienced in *Angst*—one of the fundamental existential concepts, as we have already found in Kierkegaard. This *Angst* or dread reveals the emptiness of all the multiple things in which a man has hitherto been interested and shows up the "Nought" (*Nichts*), the nothingness behind it.

This is the moment when Kierkegaard's spirit felt giddy and made the "leap" into the religious sphere, to God. For Heidegger there is no such solution. Man must empty to the dregs the chalice of the bitter experience that he is "being held into the Nought." For he is "thrown" into existence without knowing who or what has thrown him, so his origin is lost in the Nought; the things around him have already revealed their "Nought," and he cannot be sure whether his own possibilities will ever be realized; the only possibility that is sure to be actualized is the possibility of death—but death is the fall into the abyss, into the Nought. And so all life is "existence unto death" —*Dasein zum Tode*. The man who exists "authentically" will accept, even "will," this situation that is on all sides surrounded by the "Nought." Later Heidegger has somewhat modified his standpoint and described man as the "shepherd of being," entrusted with the "guardianship of being," but exactly what this means I must confess I do not know. The whole tenor of his philosophy is no doubt thoroughly pessimistic, for an existence that is a "thrownness" from the Nought into the Nought can have no meaning at all, whether the man thus "thrown" is a shepherd of being (and what precisely is meant by "being" in this context?) or not.

Jean Paul Sartre

If Heidegger is the characteristic representative of the dark musings of the Teutonic existentialist spirit, Jean Paul Sartre is the exponent of the corresponding French mentality. In contrast with the German thinker, he is not only a philosopher, but also a successful novelist and dramatist; but all his works whether philosophical or imaginative express his fundamental pessimism.

As a philosopher Sartre divides Being into two kinds, the "being in itself" (the *en-soi*), which is unconscious, opaque, altogether one with itself, and the "being for itself," (the *pour-soi*), conscious being, that is a less opaque being, the fullness of which is broken by the "Nothing" and which is burdened with freedom. In Sartre's view, consciousness, far from being a superior form of being, is on the contrary a lowering, because it is caused by the "nothing," which brings about, as it were, a rent or fissure in the "being in itself." So the "nothing" is a constituent factor in conscious being, and this "nothing" prevents a man from being completely himself in the way that unconscious being, the *en-soi*, is itself. Thus man is always striving to become himself, to create himself and the values by which he is to live, for his freedom is unlimited, and he has to make his decisions in utter loneliness, hence, once again, in "dread" (*angoisse*). But this striving to become himself never reaches its goal, for it is impossible to be both *en-soi* and *pour-soi*, and so man, defined by classical thought as a "rational animal," is for Sartre a "useless passion."

It is not surprising that the fundamental mood of a man holding such a view of the world should be disgust; and it is only fitting that Sartre's best-known novel should be called *La Nausée (Nausea)*, for a world devoid of meaning in which man is condemned to live and make decisions without the help of any values or principles, in total "freedom," is indeed apt to produce a feeling of nausea.

In this novel the essence of Sartre's philosophy is expressed in the famous scene in the municipal gardens where the hero, Antoine Roquentin, experiences a sort of existentialist "ecstasy"—in fact Sartre himself uses this term, which is normally reserved for a mystical state. While contemplating the root of a tree, Roquentin realizes that "we were a mass of existence, troubled, obstructed by ourselves, we had not the least reason to be there, neither the ones nor the others; each existing thing, confused and vaguely uneasy, felt itself to be 'too much' (*de trop*) in relation to the others. Too much: this was the only relation I could establish between these trees, these iron railings, these pebbles. . . . And I . . . I, too, was too much. . . . I dreamt vaguely to suppress myself, in order to annihilate at least one of these superfluous existences. But my death itself would have been 'too much' . . . I was too much for all eternity. . . . The word Absurdity is now formed by my pen. . . . I realized that I had found the clue to existence, the clue of my own nausea, of my own life. In fact, all that I have been able to grasp afterwards reduces itself to that fundamental absurdity. . . . Just now I have had the experience of the absolute. The absolute or the absurd. . . . The world of explanations and reasons is not that of existence. A circle is not absurd, it can be quite well explained . . . but then a circle does not exist. This root, on the other hand, existed in proportion as I could not explain it. . . . This moment was extraordinary. I was there, motionless and paralyzed, plunged into a horrible ecstasy. But, in the very heart of this ecstasy something new had appeared; I understood the Nausea, I possessed it. . . . The essential thing is contingence. I mean that, by definition, existence is not necessary. There are people . . . who have understood this. Only they have tried to overcome this contingence by inventing a necessary being which is its own cause. But no necessary being can explain existence: contingence is the absolute, consequently perfect gratuitousness."

Sartre himself calls this "ecstasy" horrible, for it defies all man's aspirations by depriving him and the world of any meaning whatsoever. Hence it is only consistent that love, too, is meaningless. After a long analysis of the psychology of generosity in his principle philosophical work, *L'Être et le Néant* (Being and Nothingness) Sartre concludes: "To give is to enslave," because by the gift I make to another I necessarily wish to destroy the other's liberty and to subject him. For every man is, as it were, enclosed in his own liberty, and by involving him, through a gift in gratitude, his liberty is diminished, as it is, indeed, even by the presence of other men. As, in Sartre's view, liberty is the very essence of man, love is the desire to possess the other's liberty. When these two liberties meet, the result is not communion but conflict. Thus to love means to lose one's own liberty by destroying that of the other. The relation between Roquentin and Anny in *La Nausée*, which is one of constant conflict ending in utter futility and disappointment, is the typical presentation of Sartre's concept of "love." Nevertheless, Sartre does not draw from his teaching the obvious conclusion that man in the loneliness of his absurd existence should either commit suicide or throw himself into a whirlpool of dissipation in order to forget the tragic predicament of his existence. He teaches on the contrary that man must endure and master this inevitable mood in heroic self-assertion. He himself joined the Resistance movement and later, like so many misguided French intellectuals, the Communist party—so he is certainly not without interest in the social and political problems of our time. But if man is really this futile individual closed in upon himself, without love for God or his fellows, without any objective standards by which to rule his life, it is hard to see why he should behave just like those whose philosophy is diametrically opposed to his. Could it be that, after all, Sartre's own life proves that his thought is wrong?

Albert Camus

If there is absurdity in existence as it presents itself to the mind of Sartre, this element is elevated into a principle by another French thinker, Albert Camus. Less of a professional philosopher than Sartre, the ideas of Camus are propagated mainly in highly successful plays and novels, and he has recently been awarded the Nobel Prize for literature. His ideas can be reduced to two tenets;

there is no God, and life is absurd. In *Cross Purpose (Le Malentendu)* the Mother says: "This world doesn't make sense," and after she and her daughter have unknowingly killed their own son and brother, the daughter tells his widow: "Pray your God to harden you to stone. It's the happiness He has assigned Himself, and the one true happiness. Do as He does, be deaf to all appeals and turn your heart to stone. . . . You have the choice between the mindless happiness of stones and the slimy bed [i.e. of the river] in which we are awaiting you."

Camus realizes of course that most men simply cannot live in such a world. As Cherea says in the third act of *Caligula:* "I like, and need, to feel secure. So do most men. They resent living in a world where the most preposterous fancy may at any moment become a reality, and the absurd tranfix their lives. . . . I want to know where I stand, and to stand secure." And Caligula answers: "Security and logic don't go together." For the atheist existentialist, the absurdity of the world is the result of logic —*his* logic. And it is his "morality" to go on living in this world with the full knowledge of the absurdity of life, a kind of perverted heroism.

For strangely enough Camus is deeply interested in the question of how to be a saint, one of the chief subjects of his novel *La Peste*. While the plague rages in a town in North Africa, Dr. Rieux treats the sick with the devotion of a saint. When his friend Tarrou asks him why he does so seeing he does not believe in God, Rieux replies that, if he believed in an almighty God he would leave the care of the sick to Him. But nobody really believes in such a God because nobody abandons himself completely to Him; therefore he, Rieux, believes to be on the right way by fighting against creation such as it is: "Because the order of the world is regulated by death, it is perhaps better for God not to believe in Him but to fight with all one's powers against death, without raising one's eyes to heaven where He is silent."

In a later conversation Tarrou comes back to this subject. "In short . . . what interests me is to know how one becomes a saint." "But you do not believe in God." "Exactly, can one be a saint without God? This is the sole problem I know today."

A climax is reached when a small boy dies in atrocious suffering after all the efforts of the doctors have failed to keep him alive. Rieux exclaims: "I shall refuse until death to love this creation where children are tortured." But this deathbed has not only shocked Rieux, it has also seriously upset a Jesuit, Père Paneloux, who has watched it. At the beginning of the plague he had preached a sermon in which he presented the calamity as a divine punishment. After the death of the child he has changed completely. The Christian, he said, must face an essential choice. "We must admit the scandal, because we must choose between hating or loving God. And who would dare to hate God? . . . This is the faith, cruel in the eyes of men, decisive in the eyes of God, which we must approach. We must come up to this terrible image." A few days later the Jesuit dies, desperately clutching his crucifix, apparently in a state of mental derangement.

Tarrou, the man who wanted to be a saint without God, also dies, one of the last victims of the plague. "Tarrou had lived in anguish and contradiction, he had never known hope. . . . A warmth of life and an image of death, this was knowledge."

And, when the plague has finally ceased, Rieux sums up the meaninglessness of it all: "He thought that it is unimportant whether the things have a meaning or not, but that one must see only to what corresponds to the hope of men. . . . If there is one thing that one can always desire and sometimes obtain, it is human tenderness. . . . For those, on the other hand, who had turned above man to something they could not even imagine, there had been no response. . . . And Rieux thought that it was just that, at least from time to time, joy should recompense those who were content with man and his poor and terrible love."

There is nothing beyond man; a little human tenderness, if it be met, is the most we can expect from life, nothing else makes sense. The plague, it is true, is over in that city, "but he knew what the joyous crowds did not, . . . that the germ of the plague never disappears, that it can remain dormant for decades . . . and that, perhaps, the day would come, when . . . the plague would revive its rats and send them to die in a happy city."

Jean Anouilh

Another successful French author takes an even gloomier view of "existence." Anouilh's personages frankly refuse to face the difficulties of grown-up life, for them there is not even "human tenderness" to redeem the absurdity of man's presence in the world. The author chooses the classical subject of Antigone as a mouthpiece of his ideas. Like the figure in the play of Sophocles, Antigone tries to bury the body of her rebellious brother against the strict orders of her uncle Creon, who has forbidden his subjects under pain of death to give the dead man this last honor. But, unlike the Greek heroine, the modern Antigone, who behaves throughout like a hysterical flapper, does not believe at all in the religious significance of her act, and for a moment even lets herself be persuaded by Creon that her venture is senseless, because both her brothers, the one who is honored by a state funeral and the other who is refused any burial at all were equally guilty. But then Creon, who is trying to save her, and who represents the disillusioned wisdom of middle age, makes a fatal mistake. "Life," he tells her "is nothing more than the happiness that you get out of it." That calls forth Antigone's outburst: "I spit on your happiness! I spit on your idea of life—that life that must go on, come what may. . . . I want everything of life, I do; and I want it now! I want it total, complete: otherwise I reject it . . . I want to be sure of everything this very day; sure that everything will be as beautiful as when I was a little girl. If not, I want to die."

It is the final refusal to grow up, to come to maturity. There is nothing but the defiant: "I want . . . " of the individual who realizes that life as it is will never give him the absolute that he wants; simply because life is not lived in isolation. This realization leads to total hatred expressed even more intransigently in Anouilh's *Orpheus*: "I hate them all, every one of them, so let nobody come and try to make of their million sorrows a big sister of compassion for me. Each of us is alone. Each is quite alone. That is the one thing certain."

It is the same in most other plays of Anouilh. In *The Waltz of the Toreadors*, which has a modern setting, General St. Pé, an old roué with a neurotic wife, explains to Gaston, his secretary, who later turns out to be his illegitimate son, his philosophy of life: all is really quite meaningless: the only thing one can do is to keep on swimming in the sea watching the lifebuoy (representing a more or less religious belief that prevents despair), yet, if one tries to reach it by deliberately setting out for it one will inevitably drown. The best thing of all is to swim towards it together with a woman one loves. In the course of the play the general himself loses the woman he has loved for seventeen years, and never possessed, to his son—and goes off with the housemaid to resume his ordinary life. Not that he really enjoys this kind of thing, but "because it is not so lonely in the dark." Here, too, life is sheer disillusionment, utterly absurd; love either does not exist or is doomed to frustration; there may be some "lifebuoy" somewhere, but it is better not to strain towards it, or it will be lost altogether. Thus life, in the plays of Anouilh, appears as one great puberty crisis that leaves man only the choice between premature death and the disillusioned, despicable compromises of middle age, without even the faint glow of human tenderness that lights up the absurd world of Albert Camus.

Prophets of Gloom

We have quickly passed in review some of the most influential representatives of the view of life and the world that is generally called existentialism, and no doubt the reader of the preceding pages, like the author, will have been left with a bitter taste in his mouth. It may seem strange that a profoundly religious man like Kierkegaard should have had such a large atheistic posterity (we shall discuss his Christian followers in the next chapter), yet this is not so odd as it looks at first sight. As we have seen, for Kierkegaard the existence of God was not an objective reality that could be apprehended by human reason but a matter of personal choice. If a man, in the grip of dread because he finds himself involved in sin decides to take the "leap" into the religious sphere, he will find himself in the realm of the "absolute paradox," alone with his God, and all will be well. But if he does not take this leap . . . the outcome we have seen in Heidegger and Sartre, Camus and Anouilh.

If a man endowed with the normal human equipment of common sense immerses himself in the world of the existentialist authors, especially in their plays and novels which are more readily accessible than their large philosophic tomes on existence, nothingness and the rest, he will feel as if he were living in a nightmare world. The persons are no real human beings of flesh and blood living in this world, but seem rather like the damned after the General Resurrection, endowed with bodies that are but instruments increasing the torment of the soul inside.

They all might make their own the horrible words of Anouilh's Antigone: "We are of the tribe that hates your filthy hope, your docile, female hope; hope, your harlot."

How is it possible that men who are not even downs-and-outs but highly successful authors, should take such a view of life? What seems to me the principal point that is wrong with them and which they share with Kierke-gaard himself, is their utter contempt for human reason. For Kierkegaard, reason had nothing at all to do with religion, in fact could only be harmful to it; whereas Sartre sees in consciousness—which non-existentialist thinkers regard as a higher form of being—actually a diminution of this brute, undifferentiated being which throws Antoine Roquentin into ecstasy when contemplat-ing the root of a tree. For Camus life is absurd, without a purpose, hence human reason can only abdicate before its meaninglessness; Anouilh considers the growth of understanding that accompanies maturity as a loss com-pared with the irrational enthusiasm of adolescence. For one and all of them happiness, which is the final end of man, and which he pursues througout his life however mistaken his idea of it may be, is something completely illusory. Man's existence is without meaning, there is neither hope nor happiness; yet he must pursue this sense-less life, indeed "engage" himself in it while fully realiz-ing that it leads to nothing. Why he should do so rather than himself put an end to such a hopeless existence is evidently easier to see for existentialists than for their less perspicacious fellowmen.

It is, however, remarkable, that existentialists display a truly missionary zeal in propagating their views by a flood of literature, only a few specimens of which have been selected for the present study. And, what is perhaps even more remarkable, is the astounding success their apostolate of pessimism has had in the non-Catholic and, indirectly, even in the Catholic world. Their novels are mostly best-sellers, translated into many languages, their plays draw full houses in Europe as well as in the States. It is not enough to shake one's head and leave it at that, else the poison will continue to spread. On the other hand, all too sympathetic studies of the existentialist disease will inject the virus into one's own mind; it is surely a disquieting sign that a prominent Catholic theologian should demand a new branch of theology devoted solely to *Angst,* as does Urs von Balthasar in his study on the subject. If Christians would enter into discussion with existentialists they must do so not in the name of dread but under the banner of Hope. But by hope we mean not the debased conception of Anouilh that is but the weak "bourgeois" compromise with the mediocrity of a life from which not only Christian faith but even pagan ideals are totally absent; the hope which alone can defeat our modern gloom is that which St. Paul knew to be one of the great triad of Christian virtues: Faith, Hope and Charity, the hope whose great hero is Abraham "who against hope believed in hope" (Rom. 4:18), a hope which is not the cowardly refusal to face despair but the Christian fortitude of mind which, as St. Paul says in the same Letter (5:4f.) is born in trials and can never be shaken because it springs from our love of God which the Holy Spirit has poured into our hearts.

It is significant that several decades before Camus invented his Père Paneloux whose faith and hope collapsed at the deathbed of somebody else's child, a Christian father described his and his wife's reactions to the death of their own child: "Confronted by the death of a small child, Art and Poetry are truly like the deepest wretchedness. . . . Yet there is no sorrow other than that which is told in Your Book (i.e. the Bible). . . . Seek as we will, not a single sorrow shall we find outside the circle of fire of the revolving Sword which guards the lost Garden. Every affliction of body or soul is an evil of exile, and the devastating compassion bestowed upon little tiny coffins is surely that which most compellingly recalls the famous Banishment for which mankind, stripped of innocence, has never been able to console itself. . . . One sole word was uttered, the word Blessing, which fell from the lips of the mother. . . . However much they might suffer from now on . . . they were sure nonetheless that something of themselves was shining in blessed glory beyond the worlds." Thus wrote Léon Bloy after the death of his child. (*La Femme Pauvre*, cited from Raissa Maritain's *Pilgrim of the Absolute*.)

The fact of the matter is that the existentialists are quite right: without belief in God such suffering is absurd, senseless, totally incomprehensible. Camus, too, is right: if man has reason, and if the happenings in the world do not make sense to his reason (as we must admit they don't unless we believe in God) then everything is absurd. But the presupposition of it all is that there is no God. And the atheist existentialists are right once again if they refuse to take the "leap" into Kierkegaard's sphere of the "absolute paradox" since, in the Danish thinker's own view, such a leap depends on choice. If God and all His existence implies is a matter of personal choice—well, then we cannot be blamed if we avail ourselves of our freedom to choose or not to choose and opt against His existence.

If God and man are totally divorced from each other, because God is wholly inaccessible to man, and man must "leap" right out of his own sphere of a rational being and by an act of personal choice apprehend that God who is the absolute paradox—then, indeed, everything may happen. We may either not take the leap at all because our spirit feels so "giddy" with dread, as Kierkegaard describes it, that it refuses to cast itself into the abyss, or this leap may take us into the sphere of the "absolute paradox"—which, however, may not be reality at all but a figment of our own imagination. This is, indeed, extremely likely if we profess with Kierkegaard that "truth is subjectivity." If truth is subjectivity, the word truth is completely emptied of its meaning; if things are true only for myself then the ravings of a diseased mind are as true as the proposition that twice two are four. If we start from these premises then it is really not surprising that we should end in a world where consciousness is distinguished from Being by Nothing and the Absurd is the ultimate "meaning" of life.

Happily this topsy-turvy world of existential thought is not the real world. It is significant that existentialism has had its greatest success in France, and, secondly, in Germany—both countries which have greatly suffered in the two world wars. More; both in Germany and in France eighteenth century rationalism had made deep

inroads into the religious faith of these countries, and in
the nineteenth century, for reasons that cannot be discussed here, the Protestant Church in Germany and the
Catholic Church in France had almost completely lost
their hold both on the intellectuals and on the masses of
industrial workers. They retained practically only the
bourgeois middle classes which, in their turn, regarded
Christianity as not very much more than an adjunct of
respectable life like having family portraits on the walls
and carpets in the drawing room. Of course this is a
generalization, but by and large it is, I think, a fairly
adequate description of the *general* situation on the Con-
tinent of Europe.

The two great wars of 1914 and 1939 and their after-
math completely shook European man's faith in his
reason and his optimistic belief in unending human progress. Existentialism reflects the mood of profound disillusionment; it is Kierkegaard's philosophy of the hard
personal case enlarged into a philosophy of the hard
case of European man unnerved by two world wars and
the fear of a third. More, much of its attraction is probably also due to the fact that, as we shall see presently,
existentialism contains a core of perverted Christianity.

Human life is not without a meaning, as the atheist
existentialists hold, nor is Christianity the absolute paradox as Kierkegaard believed. For there is a link between
God and man, and on this link rests our hope of meeting
God, in this life and in the next. When Kierkegaard read
his Bible he must have overlooked this crucial passage
in the first chapter of the Book of Genesis: "Let us make
man to our image and likeness . . . and God created man

to his own image: to the image of God he created him."
Even the atheist existentialists are aware that man is
something extraordinary—he has consciousness, he does
not belong to brute unconscious being, as Sartre well
knows; he is capable of tenderness, the "absurdity" of the
world disquiets him, as Camus realizes so perfectly.
What is it in man that causes this *malaise,* this feeling
that he is something different, thirsting for reasonable-
ness, for justice? It is just this crucial fact that he is made
in the image of God, which distinguishes him so completely from all other creatures. But that this image does
not give him happiness but troubles him is due to the
Fall—something has gone wrong with man, and through
him with all creation. This is the experience of the existentialists, this is what causes their dread, their despair.
Man was made in the image of God, but this image has
been spoiled by the sin of the First Men. They could not
have sinned if God had not given them freedom. It would
not have been in harmony with God's love and man's dignity as a rational creature if he had had to obey God like
a robot; God gave man his freedom so that He might be
freely loved and freely obeyed. Man's sin was not a consequence, but an abuse of this freedom. The existentialists have rightly stressed man's freedom, as against the
materialistic view of Karl Marx who made man a slave of
economic laws. But they have fallen into the opposite
error and rejected the truth that man's freedom is a
divine gift and carries with it the responsibility to use it
rightly.

What is perhaps the most puzzling feature of existentialist thought is its preoccupation, or rather its obses-

sion with the "Nought," the *Nichts*, the *Rien*. This, too, is
a perversion of a Christian doctrine. If Heiddeger says
that we come from Nothing this is quite true in a sense:
for the world was created from Nothing, *ex nihilo*. We all
have this admixture of "nothingness" in our being, and
if God were to withdraw His sustaining power from us
even for an instant, we would all fall back into the
Nothing from which He created us. But as Christians we
are not confronted by this nothingness when we look at
ourselves—it is rather the "image" which we see reflected
however imperfectly, in our souls. It is this which cheers
us, gives us hope, encourages us to begin again even
when we have badly failed, though we may not be
consciously aware of it, for, as St. Paul says, being risen
with Christ in baptism we have put on the new man "who
is renewed unto knowledge, according to the image of
him who created him" (Col. 3:10). Our being, the being
of the entire universe, is drawn from nothing; more, our
human nature is fallen—this accounts for the evil in the
world and all those disturbing features which so greatly
agitate the existentialists. But we are made in the image
of God—this accounts for our reason and our free will
both so frightening to Heidegger and Sartre who feel
these endowments as a "burden"—and have rejected
them. This was the state of the pagan world before
Christ, a world in which scepticism and despair were
wide-spread and which was seen as futilely repeating
itself in endless cycles. Nevertheless, Greek philosophy,
which a second century Christian thinker, Clement of
Alexandria, considered as a kind of preparation for Christianity similar to that of the Old Testament, acknowl-

edged an intelligible world of ideas (Plato) and a divine
Mind (Aristotle's *Nous*) as the prime Mover above us,
giving meaning to human life. It is only the world of post-
Christian paganism that has elevated the meaningless of
man and his life into a philosophy—which is a contradiction in terms, because philosophy means love of wisdom. It is the ultimate consequence of rejecting the final
revelation of God in Christ and the Church: without God
everything becomes, indeed, hopeless absurdity.

2

WOMAN, SEX AND EXISTENTIALISM

Simone de Beauvoir

AFTER WHAT has been said about existentialism, this pessimistic philosophy should have little attraction for women and it is difficult to see what it could have to say on the question of feminism. Yet one of its most eminent exponents, whose books have lately found admirers also in the Anglo-Saxon world, is a woman. Simone de Beauvoir, who was born in 1908, seems in one sense to belong to the generation of Mrs. Pankhurst and the English suffragettes rather than to her own. In her most important non-fiction work, *The Second Sex,* she repeats all the old slogans of the absolute equality of men and women which we had long thought buried. What is new is that she dresses them up in an up-to-the-minute terminology in which every human being must needs be called an "existent" and juggles with the *en-soi* and the *pour-soi,* with "Immanence" and "transcendence" (in the Sartrian sense, of course), till the hapless reader wonders what all this jargon has got to do with her subject.

31

For the fact is that it has very little if any connection with it but that, if one wants to be taken seriously by our contemporaries, one has to use these peculiar terms. Nevertheless, it does seem odd that Mademoiselle de Beauvoir, of all people, should see fit to embellish her book with them. For the whole thesis of her work is that woman is intellectually equal to man, but doomed to frustration because she has to live in a world dominated by man and masculine thought. If once her social position were changed and she were regarded as man's equal, she would bring forth just as original systems of thought, forms of art and culture as men. It would seem that the least Beauvoir could have done would have been to produce her own philosophy to fit these ideas—instead of which she quite uncritically takes over the philosophy of her master, Sartre, lock, stock and barrel. And, as if this were not enough, she bolsters up her highly unoriginal views with another product of the male mind, psychoanalysis, mixing its terminology with that of Sartre into a very confused and highly indigestible hodgepodge.

If women are often accused of being illogical and "thinking with their emotions," this is unfortunately only too true of Mademoiselle de Beauvoir. In fact, *The Second Sex* is dominated by what her countrymen call *ressentiment*—by a permanent grievance at having been born a woman. "Legislators, priests, philosophers, writers and scientists," she writes, "have striven to show that the subordinate position is willed in heaven and advantageous on earth. The religions invented by men reflect this wish for domination. In the legends of Eve and Pandora men have taken up arms against women" (p. 21). But it is not only men who have taken up arms against unfortunate womankind, it is nature itself. Simone de Beauvoir describes the physical phenomena to which the female body is subject in the most lurid colors—it is truly remarkable that the female sex should have survived in strength, menaced as it is by "the conflict between species and individual, which ... endows the feminine body with a disturbing frailty" (p. 58). For though "woman, like man, *is* her body," yet "her body is something other than herself" (p. 57). It is difficult, indeed, to follow the author's logic. If woman is her body, that is, if she and her body are identical (which is a statement unacceptable to anyone not professing a materialistic philosophy) how can it at the same time be "other than herself"? But there are even more extraordinary statements to come. "Woman," Mademoiselle de Beauvoir writes, "is a female to the extent that she feels herself as such. . . . It is not nature that defines woman; it is she who defines herself by dealing with nature on her own account in her emotional life" (p. 65). Here we have Sartre's concept of freedom applied to natural fact—and the result is quite simply raving nonsense. If a woman is not female by nature but "defines herself as such" what is she—male, or neuter? And is man, perhaps, male only because he "defines himself as such"? In the author's view "the worst curse that was laid upon woman was that she should be excluded from these warlike forays" of primitive tribes, according to Beauvoir herself, on account of her weaker nature, though this flatly contradicts her earlier statement that woman is only "a female to the extent that she feels herself as such;" and she triumphantly concludes that "an existentialist perspective has enabled us . . . to understand how the biological and economic condition of the primitive horde must have led to male supremacy. . . . It is because humanity calls itself in question in the matter of living—that is to say, values the reasons for living above mere life—that, confronting woman, man assumes mastery. . . . It is male activity that in creating values has made of existence itself a value; this activity has prevailed over the confused forces of life; it has subdued Nature and Woman" (p. 90f.). Frankly, I fail to understand this existentialist explanation of how male supremacy has come about. It is evidently based on the facts that woman is physically weaker than man, has to bear children and so forth, but then Beauvoir has just said: "Certainly these facts cannot be denied—but in themselves they have no significance." If facts have no significance, what has? And evidently even she admits that they were sufficiently significant to subject woman to man in the life of the "primitive horde."

A few pages later, however, she has forgotten the horde and blandly states that "the oppression of woman has its cause in the will to perpetuate the family and to keep patrimony intact." For the family is Beauvoir's enemy number one, since it prevents the freedom of woman as well as free love. "If marriage was held to be an institution demanding mutual fidelity, it seemed obvious that the wife should be totally subordinated to her husband: through St. Paul the Jewish tradition, savagely anti-feminist, was affirmed" (p. 120). The author's lack of logic is matched only by her ignorance, for there were few races in the ancient world who accorded a higher po-

sition to women than the Jews. The Fathers of the
Church, she asserts, continue the tradition; she unfortunately cites especially Tertullian, who was not a "Father of the Church" but became a Montanist, a member
of a heretical sect professing exaggerated moral doc-
trines. She further quotes an isolated passage from Chry-
sostom—unluckily for her one of the Fathers least in-
clined to frown on the female sex, whose own intimate
friendship with the deaconess Olympias should surely
have saved him from being referred to in this context.
After informing us that "all the Fathers of the Church
proclaimed her [woman's] abjectly evil nature" (p. 122)
the author says on the very next page that "It is sure that
the Church exalted the cult of the mother of the Re-
deemer to such a degree that we can say that in the
thirteenth century God had been made woman." How
this hair-raising nonsense is to be reconciled with the
previous statement about woman's abjectly evil nature
is best known to Mademoiselle de Beauvoir; but we may
be pardoned if such absurdities prevent us from taking
her as seriously as many of her admirers. It is, however,
essential to cite one more passage of the work dealing
with Christianity because it presents fallacies that are
very common among our contemporaries and which, as
we shall see, have infiltrated even into the work of Christian authors. She writes: "It is Christianity which invests
woman anew with frightening prestige: fear of the other
sex is one of the forms assumed by the anguish of man's
uneasy conscience. The Christian is divided within himself; the separation of body and soul, of life and spirit, is
complete; original sin makes of the body the enemy of the

soul; all ties of the flesh seem evil. Only as redeemed by Christ and directed towards the kingdom of heaven can man be saved; but originally he is only corruption: his birth dooms him not only to death but to damnation . . . in all the forms of his natural existence there is a curse. Evil is an absolute reality; and the flesh is sin. And of course, since woman remains always the Other, it is not held that reciprocally male and female are both flesh: the flesh that is for the Christian the hostile *Other* is precisely woman. In her the Christians find incarnated the temptations of the world, the flesh and the devil" (p. 185).

Here we have as it were in a nutshell all the frightful ideas resulting from the seventeenth century heresy of Jansenism which can be traced even in the works of Catholic writers such as Mauriac and Graham Greene. There is first of all the fear of sex, which takes no account of the Scriptural creation story, according to which God made man in two sexes and saw that all he had made "was very good." Secondly, the dichotomy of body and soul is held to involve complete separation, whereas, quite on the contrary, the body is destined to share the glory of the soul after the General Resurrection so that the two are, indeed, inseparable. Thirdly, original sin does not make the body the enemy of the soul, though unfortunately the language of certain saints and spiritual writers might lead to this error. In fact, by upsetting the original equilibrium of the human being, original sin has made it more difficult for the soul to subject the desires of the body to reason and will. Man is not "originally only corruption"—this is rank Calvinism, nor does his birth doom him to damnation. For the Christian, the only "absolute reality" is God; evil, far from being "absolute" is something negative; from the very first century of the Christian era the Church has always condemned the dualist heresies which made evil an uncreated reality on a par with God. Nor has the Church ever taught that the flesh is sin—how could she, seeing that the flesh was made by God, and that both Christ Himself, the Godman, and His sinless Mother had bodies of flesh?

"And, of course, since woman remains always the Other, it is not held that reciprocally male and female are both flesh, the flesh that is for the Christian the hostile Other is precisely woman." It seems almost incredible that an otherwise highly educated woman should make such preposterous statements. First of all, this concept of "the Other" is an existentialist term which has no relevance to Christian thought at all. Secondly, if the author had troubled to look up the first chapters of Genesis she would have found there Adam's quite unequivocal statement: "This (that is the newly created woman) now is bone of my bones, and flesh of my flesh. . . . Wherefore a man shall leave father and mother, and shall cleave to his wife; and they shall be two in one flesh" (Gen. 2:23f.). Then, to top it all, Beauvoir declares: "The aversion of Christianity in the matter of the feminine body is such that while it is willing to doom its God to an ignominious death, it spares Him the defilement of being born: the Council of Ephesus in the Eastern Church and the Lateran Council in the West declare the virgin birth of Christ" (p. 185). This, surely, is the *non plus ultra*, one does not know whether to say of ignorance or of impudent lying; but even a disciple of Sartre might have known that the whole Christian world celebrates the birth of Christ as one of its greatest feasts. In fact, if we would be as perverse as Beauvoir, we might state the exact opposite with far greater justification and say that "the aversion of Christianity in the matter of the masculine body is such that . . . it spares Him the defilement of a human father!" It might be said that the Church positively exalts the feminine body in an unheard-of manner by teaching all its members to pray many times every day: "Blessed is the fruit of thy womb, Jesus." How the doctrine of the Virgin birth can be thought to mean that Christianity "spares Him the defilement of being born" defies comprehension; and, of course, the Virgin birth was not defined by the Council of Ephesus (A.D. 431), since it is plainly taught already in the New Testament; what was defined at Ephesus was that Mary was truly Mother of God, which, in Greek, is *Theotokos,* a term which expresses much more strongly than the English translation the very act of giving birth.

All this incredible misrepresentation of Christian teaching on the part of a highly educated Frenchwoman, coming from a practicing Catholic family, who need only have looked up a theological dictionary or consulted any priest or knowledgeable layman on the subject to put her right, springs from a quite obvious psychological source: a deep-seated hatred of Christianity and all it stands for inextricably entangled with her resentment of being a woman. Christianity, following the obvious natural data expressing woman's God-given place in creation, assigns to her as her principle task motherhood and the building up of the family under the protection of her husband.

This is her normal and primary vocation. But the Church
has always recognized that there are also other possible
vocations; first of all the strictly religious one, in which
many highly gifted women have found full scope for their
abilities; Beauvoir herself is a sincere admirer of St. Teresa of Avila, a strange choice, indeed, seeing that Teresa
had a very low opinion of her own sex. But outstanding
personalities like St. Catherine of Siena and St. Joan of
Arc invaded even the masculine world of politics and
war, and the spheres of writing, painting and music have
always been open to women if they had sufficient talent
and energy. But there's the rub. Throughout the thousands of years of human civilization there have only been
very few women outstanding in the spheres of art and
scholarship, and none to equal the great masculine geniuses, a Shakespeare or Rembrandt or Dante. Carefully
avoiding the simple explanation that woman, after all,
may have a different vocation from man, Beauvoir gives
us her own existentialist interpretation: "Art, literature,
philosophy, are attempts to found the world anew on a
human liberty: that of the individual creator; to entertain
such a pretension one must first unequivocally assume the
status of a being who has liberty. The restrictions that
education and custom impose on woman now limit her
grasp on the universe" (p. 669). These are very clever
sounding words—but what do they mean? First of all, that
art etc. are "attempts to found the world anew on a human
liberty" is a very odd definition which may perhaps suit
some modern art forms but which is certainly not ap-
plicable to art and scholarship as such. But it is more than
doubtful that all creative men first "unequivocally as-

sumed the status of a being who has liberty." There were many geniuses who lived in circumstances almost wholly deprived of liberty, who had the energy to educate themselves though all the odds were against them, and laboriously worked their way to the heights. There have been many women, too, who became well-known writers; there was surely nothing in their external circumstances that would explain why, say, the emancipated Madame de Staël or George Eliot did not become a Dostoevski or a Balzac, an Ibsen or a Shaw.

The most destructive and pernicious part of the book, however, is the section devoted to the married woman. Beauvoir's hatred of marriage is as deeply ingrained as her hatred of Christianity. She brutally mocks man's ideal of woman as the homemaker, the preserver of life, which she holds to be a degrading vocation. A happy marriage seems to her a contradiction in terms. "Even when the woman is young there is a hoax in marriage, since, while being supposed to socialize eroticism, it succeeds only in killing it." (p. 202), or again: "The aim of marriage is in a way to immunize a man against *his own* wife: but other women keep—for him—their heady attraction" (p. 203). It certainly is an extraordinary aim that Beauvoir assigns to marriage, but worse is to come. "Marriage," Beauvoir says, "is obscene in principle in so far as it transforms into rights and duties those mutual relations which should be founded on a spontaneous urge" (p. 432). Here we are at the center of the existentialist conception, or rather misconception, of marriage. For existentialism, and especially Sartrian existentialism, by emphasizing its particular idea of freedom as the liberty, and,

indeed, the duty to follow every urge whatever its consequences, denies the very roots of all—not only Christian—society. Because the sexual act is primarily designed to propagate the human race and hence bound
up with the life of society it must be subject to certain
laws. This is utterly repulsive to Simone de Beauvoir; for
whom the sexual act is, to put is quite crudely, a means of
amusement: the fact that it may result in the production
of children is most unfortunate, and she strongly urges
that women should be fully instructed in all the methods
of contraception, so that they may give full rein to their
passions without having to fear the consequences. "What
bourgeois optimism has to offer the engaged girl," she
writes, "is certainly not love; the bright ideal held up to
her is that of happiness, which means the ideal of quiet
equilibrium in a life of immanence and repetition" (p.
434). To oppose love to happiness is certainly an odd
idea; contradicting the most fundamental human instinct
that seeks love precisely for the happiness it brings. But
then Beauvoir has a peculiar idea of happiness, too: "A
gilded mediocrity lacking ambition and passion, aimless
days indefinitely repeated, life that slips away gently towards death without questioning its purpose—this is
what is meant by 'happiness'" (p. 435). And so she paints
the terrifying image of the existentialist bride: "In the
solitude of her new home, bound to a man who is more
or less a stranger to her, no longer a child but a wife
destined to become a mother in her turn, she feels a
chill . . . lost in a world where no future calls, abandoned
in an icy present, she becomes aware of the ennui and
the flat dullness of pure and empty sham" (p. 444).

What are Beauvoir's authorities for this dismal view of marriage? The diary of the young Countess Tolstoy (surely no "bourgeoise"!), the novels of Colette and Marcel Prévost and the journal of a psychiatrist! Indeed most of the illustrations of her book are taken from either specially selected literary or psycho-analytical sources, and with this one-sided material at her disposal she has little difficulty to affirm that marriage has been "perverted from the start" (p. 463). What, then, is to take its place? "The ideal . . . would be for entirely self-sufficient human beings to form unions one with another only in accordance with the untrammelled dictates of their mutual love" (p. 456). Here we are once more at the root of the existentialist delusion. For no human being can ever be "entirely self-sufficient," every man and woman depends on thousands of other human beings, natural circumstances and spiritual influences, which is a simple fact quite independent of any religious convictions. Moreover, even if there were an "entirely self-sufficient" human being, once he formed a union with another—would he then still be "entirely self-sufficient"? Would not his very union with another destroy his self-sufficiency? And, unless Simone de Beauvoir desired the destruction of the human race, such unions would result in offspring, and would not this imply at least some quite elementary ties and responsibilities?

"The tragedy of marriage," she continues, "is not that it fails to assure woman the promised happiness" (existentialists have a neurotic aversion against happiness, at least against that of others) "but that it mutilates her; it dooms her to repetition and routine" (p. 462). But then most of life is repetition and routine—not only for the married woman but also for the career woman. The daily round of the doctor, the school mistress, the business woman involves just as much routine and sometimes even more than that of the housewife. And what about men? After having constantly bemoaned on the first 591 pages that woman is doomed to "immanence," boredom, repetition, routine, while man is the master of his destiny, conquering the world, and enjoying his "transcendence," suddenly, on page 592, Beauvoir has to admit that man's life is not so very different after all: "The men of the classes called precisely 'middle' implant themselves in that sphere deliberately. Destined like women to the repetition of daily tasks, identified with ready-made values, respectful of public opinion . . . the employee, the merchant, the office worker, are in no way superior to their accompanying females. Cooking, washing, managing her house . . . woman shows more initiative and independence than the man working under orders."

I must confess that throughout the author's lamentations about the futility and boredom of a woman's life I had been thinking about just this. But when I came to this passage it fairly took my breath away—for it makes nonsense of the whole argument of the book. If most men's position is no different from that of "their accompanying females," what on earth is she complaining about? Seeing she is in a quandary, she asserts that one cannot speak of "woman" in general—though she herself has done so for almost 600 pages—but only of feminine and masculine situations: "If we compare these situations rather than the people in them, we see clearly that man's is far preferable; that is to say, he has many more opportunities to exercise his freedom in the world." This is indeed true for many countries, though hardly for the Anglo-Saxon ones, but then it is by no means proved, despite certain existentialist assertions, that exercising one's freedom in the world is the primary purpose of human existence; and the catastrophes that this exercise has brought about in our century alone should give us pause. After all, if all that matters is that men—and women—should exercise their freedom we should rejoice in Hitler's and Stalin's atrocities, or Lucrezia Borgia's murders as much as in the charities of St. Vincent de Paul and the Abbé Pierre.

It is always a dangerous proceeding to think against all the evidence of facts. "Woman," says Simone de Beauvoir, "is even required by society to make herself an erotic object. The purpose of the fashions to which she is enslaved is not to reveal her as an independent individual, but rather to offer her as prey to male desires; thus society is not seeking to further her projects but to thwart them" (p. 506). Quite so. But how was it that Nina, the athletic Russian disc thrower, reared in the austere regime of hatless workaday Soviet dowdiness, was so overcome by her desire to be turned into an "erotic object" that she stole no less than five perky little hats from a London shop, thereby creating almost a political crisis? The reason is that Simone de Beauvoir, like most of her fellow existentialists, live in a totally unreal world far removed from free human "existence" about which they talk so much. The world and mankind as they appear from behind the windows of a literary café in the seventh arrondissement of Paris are not the world in which most of us live, no more than the personages of Simone de Beauvoir's outsize novel *Les Mandarins* represent more than a small section of the Paris intelligentsia. This work, found worthy of the Prix Goncourt, is the story of three women, frustrated in varying degrees, with their husbands and lovers, all of them journalists and café house politicians of semi-Communist views with plenty of money to travel, drink, and keep mistresses. Anne, the wife of an editor much older than herself, has various affairs and finally on a lecture tour in the States falls in love with Louis, an American leftist author with whom she travels but whom she leaves to return to her husband and France, though tempted to commit suicide. Her daughter, Nadine, whose seventeen year old fiancé had been killed by the Nazis, drowns her sorrow by sleeping with as many men as she can get hold of, but finally marries Henry, a journalist, after he has discarded his mistress who has devoted her whole life to him and consequently has a nervous breakdown. The rest of the book is filled up with endless political discussions, the tenor of which may be seen from a "plum" like this: "The American hegemony: this means the perpetuation of the undernourishment and oppression of all the Eastern countries; their only chance is the Soviet Union: the only chance of a humanity freed from want, slavery and stupidity is the Soviet Union; hence we must do all we can to help it," despite the labour camps, the only feature these well-fed, talkative French drawing-room communists dislike.

It is a diseased, meaningless world that the books of

Simone de Beauvoir reflect, but a world that is being taken tremendously seriously. Her outsize books are difficult to wade through; in this they are entirely different from those of her much younger countrywoman, the celebrated—or should we rather say notorious—bestselling girl novelist Françoise Sagan.

Françoise Sagan

Françoise Sagan, the daughter of a Catholic bourgeois family, born in Paris in 1935, at the time of this writing a girl of barely twenty-three, has had one of the most amazing literary careers, possible only in our world of high-pressured publicity and salesmanship. Her education was somewhat sketchy, since she resented school discipline; she was sent away from a convent school for "lack of spirituality," and later failed her final school examination several times. Her mother was furious, but her father understood her better—a situation reflected in her first book that established her fame and fortune. She wrote it during the summer holidays of 1953, and in March 1954 *Bonjour Tristesse,* the work of an eighteen year old student, was to stagger France and soon the whole literary world, enabling her to indulge her passion for high-powered cars and to make her accident in one of them front page news. What is it that made this slender novel of 126 pages (in the French edition) the unheard-of world-success it has become, having sold—till the beginning of 1958—650,000 copies in France alone, and in the United

States over a million, to say nothing of translations into
other languages and the film?

First of all, without doubt the extreme youth of its
author combined with an immense publicity drive. But
these alone are not sufficient to explain it. There must be
something in the book itself to attract these millions of
readers. Its story is simple. Its setting is the lazy, fashionable crowd holidaying on the French Riviera. The main
personage is Cécile the teenage daughter of a widower, a
well-to-do publicity agent who has just discarded his last
somewhat vulgar mistress, Elsa, and is now joined by another, the more sophisticated Anne, whom he intends to
marry. Cécile herself falls in love with Cyril, a young
man, to whom she soon gives herself in the enchantment
of a hot summer afternoon. She realizes that Anne—
though this lady sleeps with her father almost under the
eyes of his young daughter—would disapprove of her and
therefore resolves to separate the two. With a cynicism
truly frightening in the book of such a young girl, Cécile
reawakens her father's desire for his discarded mistress
by letting him meet Elsa in the company of her own
lover Cyril, and finally contrives to let Anne see Elsa in
her father's arms. Anne, outraged, departs in her car and
meets with a fatal "accident" which seems most likely to
be suicide. Cécile, though somewhat conscience-stricken
that her machinations have led to such tragic result, returns with her father to Paris, where both embark on a
new round of love affairs. Bonjour tristesse!

This is the rough outline of the story that has stirred
millions of readers, for this skeleton is richly padded with

voluptuous flesh, and the love scenes are described with a suggestiveness that might have been expected from a mature writer but is rather horrifying in the book of an eighteen year old girl. But even the youth of the author and the eroticism of her book could scarcely account for its tremendous success. There must be something else that appeals directly to contemporary readers. On the face of it *Bonjour Tristesse* must seem out of place in this study of contemporary gloom. A light-hearted story of the amours of a widower and his daughter on the Riviera— what has this to do with existentialism, *Angst* and the rest?

We have used the terms "frightening" and "horrifying" in describing its contents. And so they are. The book could, actually, only have been written in an "existential-ist" atmosphere of insecurity and "gloom." For it goes even one better than the plays of Anouilh. Anouilh's main theme is the destruction of youthful love and ideals by the bitter experiences of later life. Sagan's personages are born without ideals; having drunk in scepticism and de-spair as it were with their mother's milk, they expect nothing from life except some "affairs"—a little amuse-ment to drown the terrible *ennui* that engulfs them as soon as they are left to themselves. It seems almost in-credible that the books of Sagan, whose childhood and youth were spent during and after the Second World War, should reflect nothing whatsoever of the great social and political questions of our time. Yet this seems to be precisely one of the reasons of their success. They trans-port the reader, wearied of crises, H-bombs, and sputniks, into an adolescent dream world where all that matters is the next date with one's lover. Yet, and this gives the existential spice to these books without which they could not have had such tremendous success in the modern world, all these love affairs are enacted on a background of despair. For all the young people of her novels—Cécile in *Bonjour Tristesse*, Dominique in *Un certain sourire*, the various personages of *Dans un mois, dans un an*— suffer from a complete absence of purpose in their lives. We have seen in our previous discussions that the main thesis of existentialism is just this; whether we say with Heidegger that man is "thrown" into existence and goes to nothingness, with nought but dread and care for his companions, or with Sartre that he is a "useless passion." Françoise Sagan only draws the commonsense conclusion from this philosophy, and it is a very old one, indeed, none other than the pagan attitude St. Paul castigates in his First Letter to the Corinthians: "Let us eat and drink, for to-morrow we shall die" (15:32), only substituting "make love" for the first two verbs of the apostle.

Love-making, whether lawful or illicit, has always been the favorite theme of novelists; in Sagan's case, however, as in that of Anouilh's *Waltz of the Toreadors*, it is nothing but a momentary means for allaying the fear of existence. But in Anouilh's play it is this only for the disillusioned bon-vivant—for Sagan love-making is the drug of the despairing seventeen-year-olds. A youth breathing the atmosphere of existentialist despair and without any moral support from his elders will, except by a miracle of grace, come to this impasse. We would quote two passages, one from *Un certain sourire*, the other from *Dans un mois, dans un an* which express this attitude perfectly. "I did not refrain from smiling, I could not. Once more, I knew, I was alone. I longed to say this word to myself. Alone. Alone. But what did it matter, after all? I was a woman who had loved a man. A simple story, that. There was nothing to make a fuss about." And again: "They were sitting on a seat, it was raining all the time, and they were dead tired. She told him that she did not love him, he answered that this did not matter at all . . . And they exchanged the passionate kisses of lovers, because they were both examples of life gone wrong and it did not matter to them. Yet they loved each other in a way. And the damp cigarette which Bernard vainly tried to light was an image of their life. Because they would never be able to be really happy, and they already knew it. And, darkly, they also knew that this did not matter at all."

And so Françoise Sagan joins Simone de Beauvoir. Love is dissociated from happiness, and life is a round of futilities the boredom of which is at best interrupted by some excitement or other. But, really, neither love nor happiness matters. It is an odd philosophy to be proclaimed by a young girl of twenty-three. But because it reflects both the despair and the need for sensual enjoyment felt by so many of our contemporaries, the novels that preach it have the enormous and otherwise inexplicable success we have witnessed.

3

ANGRY YOUNG MEN

John Osborne

YOUTH and irresponsibility are factors producing best-sellers not only in France. Lately the Anglo-Saxon world, too, has been staggered by the works of some youthful authors grouped together under the name of "Angry Young Men," an appellation deriving from the tremendous Broadway success one of them, John Osborne, whose play *Look Back in Anger* was called "A minor miracle" by one of its reviewers. Jimmy Porter, its hero—if you can call him thus—is permanently angry, venting his spleen particularly on Alison his devoted wife. Her main fault, though apparently also her great attraction for him, is that she comes from an officer's family and thus belongs to a layer of society where conventions play an important part, whereas he boasts of his "low class" origin and taunts her with the prejudices of her class in constant outbursts of fury. He, too, has studied but, "angry young man" that he is, has never settled down to a normal career. At the time of the play he is running a sweet stall, but apparently his main occupation is to inveigh against the injustice of society. The author, of course, is suffi-

ciently aware of modern psychology to realize that this
a-social behavior must have a deeper cause, and in the
course of the play Jimmy informs us that his father had
been badly wounded in the Civil War in Spain, fighting,
needless to say, on the Republican side, and had come
home only to die: "For twelve months I watched my
father dying—when I was ten years old. He'd come back
from the war in Spain, you see. And certain God-fearing
gentlemen there had made such a mess of him, he didn't
have long left to live. Everyone knew it. . . . But, you see,
I was the only one who cared. . . . You see, I learnt at an
early age what it was to be angry—angry and helpless.
And I can never forget it. I knew more about love . . . be-
trayal . . . and death, when I was ten years old, than you
will probably ever know all your life."

This passage contains as it were the very essence of
Angry-Young-Manship: anger, self-pity and conceit.
There is no reasoning at all, only facile emotion. For if
Jimmy Porter and his author had stopped to think they
would have realized that there was no cause for anger:
Mr. Porter Senior had joined the Spanish revolutionaries
of his own sweet will, and the taunt against the "God-
fearing gentlemen" is quite uncalled-for, since in a war
God-fearers and atheists alike wound and kill each other;
and Jimmy's self-dramatization into a hero—the only one
who cared for his dying father—and his boasting that he
knew more about love and suffering at the tender age of
ten than others in their whole life are typical puberty
attitudes.

At the crucial moment of the play, when Alison is
afraid of telling her husband, with whom she lives in

a miserable furnished room, that she is expecting a baby, her friend Helena, represented as a pious, Church-going lady of Alison's own class, appears on the scene and is at once attacked by Jimmy. She persuades his young wife to leave him, telegraphs to her father to come and take his daughter home while Jimmy is attending a funeral, breaks the news to him when he comes back, and immediately falls into his arms. In the interval between the second and third act, Helena has become Jimmy's mistress and Alison has given birth to a still-born child and decided to go back to Jimmy. When she arrives, Helena suddenly discovers that it would be immoral to continue to live with him, leaves, and Jimmy and Alison embrace—no doubt to be angry ever after.

This, then, is "the best young play of its decade," and a "minor miracle." It is not the purpose of this book to discuss its literary merits, but only its view of life. What is its meaning and purpose? The reviewer in the London *Observer* writes that it "presents postwar youth as it really is." But does it? Is Jimmy Porter really representative of "postwar youth"? Like Françoise Sagan's personages, he is totally disillusioned almost from babyhood; he has had his decisive experience of suffering and death at the age of ten and has never changed his outlook since. So far—he is in his early twenties—his own life has been a failure; despite his evident intelligence he has no adequate work; he has married, but his relation to his wife is a kind of neurotic love-hate affair which makes them both sometimes happy and most of the time miserable. His attitude to the world is entirely negative: he is angry, full of self-pity and resentment, and his main occupation, the only one that apparently satisfies him, is to make long speeches expressing his disgust with everything and everyone. When the final curtain falls on a temporarily reconciled Jimmy and Alison there remains the impression of utter futility. None of the characters of the play has any depth—life is like that: you make love, you quarrel, you are angry, the world is unjust and you are an underdog, but there is nothing that ultimately matters, and after every new experience you go on just as before. "Postwar youth as it really is." Yet among postwar youth, are there not hundreds and thousands who become happy, mature men and women, raising families, doing work satisfying to themselves and beneficial to others, living full human lives sustained by faith, hope and charity?

But such lives rarely become subjects of our modern authors, and if they do, they fail to hit the headlines and to top the bestseller lists. For existential pessimism is the order of the day, and the positive sides of human life and character are "out."

The "angry young man" is permanently disgusted with the world and his fellowmen and considers himself superior to the "Christian" as well as the "bourgeois" who live by faith and observe the accepted standards of behavior.

Colin Wilson

But, it may be asked, has not this disgust with the world as it is, with the pettiness and materialism of human society, always been the hallmark of outstanding personalities? This is the main tenet of Colin Wilson, another "angry young man," defended in his first book *The Outsider* and its sequel *Religion and the Rebel.* The latter contains a very revealing autobiographical introduction, which provides next to no information on his family and background, but all the more about his own personality which is very like Jimmy Porter's and which he takes extremely seriously. As a boy Wilson seems to have dabbled in physics, chemistry, geology, psychology, aeronautics, philosophy and mathematics—certainly an imposing array of subjects. He read omnivorously and quite promiscuously, taking notes all the time. Once, when listening to a performance of Shaw's *Man and Superman* —he must have been thirteen or fourteen at the time—"I was astounded that another man had actually thought and written about the problems that preoccupied me. . . . It had become a commonplace of my thinking that no man asked himself what life was about; or if he did, answered with arrant nonsense or wishful thinking" (p. 19). This native conceit of the boy seems to have only increased with growing up. Seeing himself so superior it is not surprising that Wilson could not submit to the discipline of normal work: "Working in a regular job made me feel aimless, and robbed me of my sense of purpose" (p. 32). To preserve this sense intact he needed leisure; therefore: "The idea of entering a monastery also became increasingly attractive . . . the monastery symbolized serenity and time for meditation. . . . My most acute problem, I felt, was to discover a means of escaping work, escaping the complications of having to find food and drink and a change of clothes. I started instruction in

Catholicism, feeling that to become a Catholic would be the first step towards a monastery. But what I read of the strenuous life in monasteries discouraged me" (p. 28).

The naïveté of this is surely disarming. Having realized in good time that neither Catholicism ("my final disqualification . . . was my failure to see any need for Christ") nor the life of a monk would solve his particular problem, Wilson married a nurse ten years older than himself, but the marriage soon broke up. Having spent some time living as a tramp, reading in the libraries by day and sleeping in the open to save the rent, he got the idea to write a book. "Stuart Holroyd showed me the opening chapters of his *Emergence From Chaos*. Suddenly, I made a decision. I too would write a critical book—a credo. I would dash it off quickly. . . . It would be a study in various types of 'obsessed men'" (p. 38). "The success of the book winded me, and made me more certain than ever that it should have been twice as long. . . . I had believed passionately in the book, and had never doubted its importance as I wrote it" (p. 40). False humility is certainly not one of the faults of our "Angry Young Men"—but the reader of *The Outsider* may perhaps be forgiven if he is thankful the work is not twice as long, for even as it is wading through this scrapbook of extracts and notes is a very boring task.

The criticisms most often directed against his first book is that Wilson includes as "Outsiders" such diverse people as Shaw and Ramakrishna, Hermann Hesse and Dostoevski, George Fox, Schopenhauer, van Gogh, and the dancer Nijinsky and many other equally improbable se-

lections. What, then, is an "Outsider," seeing the term
which is taken from Camus' novel *L'Étranger*, is applied
to all these? It is not surprising that Wilson's explanations
should be as varied as the types covered by this term. To
give but a random selection: Taking Barbusse's *Enfer* as
his term of reference he tells us that "the Outsider is a
man who cannot live in the comfortable, insulated world
of the bourgeois, accepting what he sees and touches as
reality. He sees too deep and too much, and what he sees
is essentially *chaos*" (p. 15). "Outsiders . . . declare that
it is human nature that is sick, and the Outsider is the
man who faces that unpleasant fact" (p. 20)—incidentally a statement that covers all believing Christians.
Naturally, the fashionable term "existentialist" is not
missing, for "The Outsider tends to express himself in
Existentialist terms. He is not very concerned with the
distinction between body and spirit, or man and nature;
these ideas produce theological thinking and philosophy;
he rejects both. For him, the only important distinction
is between being and nothingness" (p. 27). It would be
interesting to learn how ideas can produce thinking, seeing that normally thinking produces ideas. It is even more
surprising that the author seems to assume that being and
nothingness are concepts absent from theology and philosophy and he would probably be astonished to learn
that they have their place not only in the existentialist
philosophy of Heidegger but in the scholastic thought of
St. Thomas.

Normally it would be a waste of time and energy to go
any further into the wealth of absurdities with which *The
Outsider* is packed; but as this book has caused such a

stir and been taken so seriously by critics and public
alike it may perhaps be useful to discuss it a little more
fully. Having said on page 27 that the Outsider is only
concerned with Being and Nothingness, no doubt under
the influence of Sartre's *L'Être et le Néant,* Wilson affirms
on page 223 that "The Outsider should be concerned with
nothing except human psychology, with discriminating
between the world as Will and the world as Delusion"—
how this is to be squared with his former statement is
hard to see, except on the very plausible assumption
that he had in the meantime come across his notes on
Schopenhauer and forgotten all about Sartre. Wilson's
use of the term "all men" is also ambiguous, for it seems
that he means by it the mass of men, all, in fact, except
the "Outsider." For "The Outsider recognizes with penetrating clearness that all men are dishonest with themselves, that all men blind themselves with their emotions"
(ch. 8), and in *Religion and the Rebel* he writes, "The
Outsider's despair . . . comes from his vision of the vast
sea of mediocrity that makes up humankind, and his re-
bellion at the idea of belonging to it" (p. 48). For "The
picture we have built up of the Outsider shows him as a
half-way house to a higher type of man . . . he loses more
sleep, eats less, and suffers from all kinds of nervous dis-
eases" (*The Outsider,* p. 183). In fact, as may have been
expected, Wilson's Outsider is a neurotic, a man who has
lost his balance—and knows it—but seeks to make up for
this loss by a fierce contempt for the "normal" man: "The
Outsider's hatred of men, his contempt for 'the life we
have lost in living,' does not become objective until he
realizes that something is wrong with the way all men

live. The ordinary businessman, the statesman, the professor, does not see man as a creature of possibilities. He sees other men as rather like himself—limited, narrow, but capable of minor achievements . . . The Outsider, with his instinctive urge to become more-than-man . . . feels the need to place man against some greater canvas than mere human beings—to see him in relation to his greatest spiritual possibilities" (*Religion and the Rebel*, p. 52). This, of course, is an unmistakable echo of Nietzsche, whom Wilson admires so much that he can write "the Night Song and the Dance Song in *Zarathustra* . . . spring out of the same emotion as . . . the Psalms of David"—a statement which Nietzsche himself would have been the first to reject with disgust.

Nevertheless, while being fully conscious of the incredible muddleheadedness of the author, it is hard to deny him all sympathy, because he is a seeker, disgusted with the materialism in which so much of our civilization is soaked, and suddenly, the smog of his musings is lit up by a flash of amazing insight: "The Outsider only exists because our civilisation has lost its religion" (*Religion*, p. 104). This, indeed, is the crux of the matter. The lack of balance, the despair, the haunting sense of the futility of life that make up the "Outsider" would vanish if he were living in a civilization that had preserved its heart, its faith in God and His Redemption.

What hinders a man like Wilson and many others of his kind from following the light they have seen for a moment? Surely the same intellectual and spiritual pride and contempt of others that prevented also the pious Pharisees from recognizing the Messias when they saw

Him. We have already cited several passages characteristic of this attitude. Here are just two more: "No amount
of logic and knowledge can make man any more than an
insect." (*Outsider*, p. 196), and, "The average man is distinguished from dogs and cats mainly because he looks
farther ahead; he is capable of worrying about his physical needs of six months hence" (p. 232). Unfortunately,
it is just this contempt of both logic and knowledge that
makes Wilson's books a mere agglomeration of names,
extracts and largely preposterous comments.

Two facts have probably contributed to the extraordinary success of this really rather boring author. One is
the title of his first book. No man likes to belong to the
crowd, a great many people fancy themselves as something out of the ordinary. Wilson himself tells us that he
received loads of letters informing him that their writers,
too, were "Outsiders." Further, this book enables readers
who would never dream of consulting a history of literature to absorb in an easy way the names and contents,
complete with commentary, of a large number of authors
and books talked about at the moment so that, after pe-
rusing it, they have the pleasant feeling of knowing all
about the trends of modern literature and thought. Unfortunately here, too, Wilson is a most unreliable guide.

We need only cite such statements as that "Newman
. . . was fundamentally very like Nietzsche" (p. 145) or,
worse, that "Christ's teaching was the same as Nietzsche's
and Buddha's" (*Religion*, p. 145), to realize that his pro-
nouncements cannot possibly be taken seriously by any
instructed person. But they are unfortunately read by
many who are not instructed, and as they are uttered with

such an impressive air of infallibility they must be re-
futed. To show that Wilson's knowledge of Christianity
is nil we may be permitted to reproduce a statement that
is rank blasphemy, but which will make it clear that all
he says on the subject is raving nonsense. He writes on
page 138 of *Religion and the Rebel:* "It soon becomes
apparent on reading the Gospels that Jesus was of the
type of the demagogue-artist; he had more in common
with Hitler than with Ramakrishna: a man of action with
a distinctly rough side to his tongue. . . . He was not . . . a
mixture of mystic and poet; in fact, he was not a mystic
at all. . . . Generally speaking, his attitude to the world
is very like Nietzsche's—harshly critical, and based on a
feeling that most men are only half-men." Surely, if, on
reading the Gospels, such a picture of our Lord can become "apparent" to a man, we may rightly assume that
everything else he reads will be similarly distorted by a
mind that sees visions of angry outsiders wherever it
looks.

So it is not surprising that Wilson takes as his two
heroes of thought two very dissimilar authors: Bernard
Shaw and Hermann Hesse. The sceptical, scintillating,
clever Irish playwright is sufficiently well-known to Eng-
lish-speaking readers to judge for themselves in how far
he can be taken seriously as a thinker; but Hermann
Hesse is an even worse choice. He is a typical product of
a kind of neo-romanticism flourishing in Germany in the
nineteen twenties, when his novels *Demian* and *Steppen-
wolf* (the latter elevated by Wilson into a kind of Outsider's Bible) made a great impression especially on the
very young, whose problems they reflected. Despite the

Nobel Prize conferred on him his books have little to recommend them to mature readers, but their descriptions of emotional tension and preoccupation with the self are just the unwholesome food for which the minds of angry young men and outsiders are craving. With Shaw and Hesse as his guiding stars Wilson passes modern literature in review, finding everywhere what he wants to find. Nietzsche, of course, holds a large place in his universe: "He has solved the body-emotions-intellect equation [whatever that may mean]. . . . He has shown that he feels the Outsider to be a prophet in disguise . . . whose salvation lies in discovering his deepest purpose, and then throwing himself into it" (p. 146); the *Brothers Karamazov* "is Dostoevski's biggest attack on the Outsider theme" (p. 178), George Fox's creed is "the Outsider's attempt to explain what has happened to him" and the "Gospel of Sri Ramakrishna" is "the only complete, exhaustive record we possess of the day-to-day utterances of a God-intoxicated saint" (p. 258).

These examples must suffice. They will have shown the confusion of the author's thought and his ignorance and, perhaps even more, the indiscriminating readiness of irresponsible reviewers and the public alike to welcome any writer who constitutes himself a rebel and a genius on his own authority. This readiness is certainly not unconnected with the growing material uniformity of our civilization and its inability to find its spiritual bearings. That there is much in our contemporary situation that gives cause for anger no thinking person would deny. But anger is a negative emotion, and it can be even more destructive if it be directed against the wrong things. The "angry young men" are wildly hitting out at anything established, an attitude not uncommon in the young. Two centuries ago the young Jean Jacques Rousseau in France denounced the very foundations of human society and preached a return to what he called "the state of nature"; under his influence Friedrich Schiller in Germany wrote his play *The Robbers*, in which a noble young man is so fed up with the pettiness of contemporary bourgeois society that he embraces the more "natural," unrestrained life of a brigand. But Schiller did not stop short at *The Robbers*. After having let off youthful steam in this play he gradually came to take a more positive view of the world as it is and settled down to become the author of such classic works as *William Tell* and *Wallenstein*. So far our Angry Young Men have shown only a few signs of outgrowing their destructive attitude. They can hardly be blamed for failing to do so, as it is just their negative, so-called existentialist view of life that has brought them fame. But anger alone cannot sustain the literary effort of a lifetime. Unless they can find a firmer basis on which to build their work they will be no more than just another symptom of the contemporary pessimistic disease, with no more than a very ephemeral success.

4

EXISTENTIALIST ATTITUDES
AND CHRISTIAN FAITH

Gabriel Marcel

THE CHURCH and her children live, in the world and in their own time, in the same surroundings as their unbelieving contemporaries. It is only natural that they should be influenced by these, that they should—consciously or unconsciously—try to come to terms with them, to achieve an outlook, a *Weltanschauung,* in which their faith blends with the tendencies of their age.

As has been seen in Kierkegaard and his twentieth century existentialist followers, the climate of modern thought is averse to the serene, abstract philosophizing of the Schoolmen; the Proofs of the Existence of God, however logical, fail to appeal to them because they appear to them as simply an intellectual exercise with little or no relevance for their day to day existence. Already Newman, whose thought had been in so many respects far in advance of his age, had felt that the time had come for a different, less theoretical approach to the data of religion and had developed in his *Grammar of Assent* the hypothesis of the "illative sense," which produces religious (and philosophical) conviction in man. In our own time a French thinker, Gabriel Marcel, also—though in a different way—combines the Christian with the "modern" approach. What gives him his special importance is not that he was brought up in Catholicism and then tried to combine it as best he could with existentialism, but that his existentialist thought led him to the Church.

We cannot, of course, give in this context even a brief outline of his thought, the more so, as, in the words of Father Copleston, "Gabriel Marcel . . . is a peculiarly elusive thinker, a philosopher whom it is extremely difficult to summarize."[1] We would only discuss a few of his ideas that have a special relevance to the subject of this book.

Like all existentialists, Marcel, too, does not consider abstract notions; for him philosophy is a concern of human "existence," of the whole human personality, not merely of the thinking mind. In his *Mystery of Being*[2] he thus describes the new type of philosopher, whom he compares with the "old" type: "This erroneous conception [i.e. of the old type] consists in imagining that the philosopher as such ought not to concern himself with passing events, that his job on the contrary is to give laws in a timeless realm. . . . I . . . think, on the contrary, that a philosophy worthy of the name ought to attach itself to a given concrete situation in order to grasp what that situation implies; and I think it should not fail to acknowledge the almost inconceivable multiplicity of combina-

---

[1] Copleston, Fredrick, *Contemporary Philosophy*, Westminster, Md.: Newman Press, 1955.
[2] Marcel, Gabriel, *Mystery of Being*, I, *Reflection and Mystery*, Chicago, Ill.: Henry Regnery Company, 1951.

tions of events that may arise from the factors it has laid
bare by its analysis" (p. 36f.). "My method of advance
does invariably consist . . . in working my way up from life
to thought and then down from thought to life again, so
that I may try to throw more light on life" (p. 41). As this
is not the traditional method of the philosopher, he, too,
uses an *ad hoc* invented terminology not found in the
philosophical textbooks. One of his fundamental distinc-
tions is that between "problem" and "mystery," the latter
term having nothing at all to do with religion. The
"problem" in his sense is something wholly objective,
which does not affect the being of the man who considers
it, such as e.g. a mathematical problem. A "mystery," on
the other hand, is something involving the personality of
the person concerned with it, which has therefore a vital
part in its solution. Hence most of the questions treated
by the old type of philosopher were really mysteries, and
it was an erroneous approach to treat them as if they
could be detached from "life" and "existence." Marcel's
own approach involves three stages: immediate experience, primary reflection, and secondary reflection. In
The Mystery of Being he applies this threefold approach
to existence itself: "When I say, not that I am, but that
I exist . . . I glimpse more or less the fact that my being is
not only present to my own awareness but that it is a
manifest being. . . . This awareness is expressed in the
small child by cries, by leaps and so on. . . . Primary reflection . . . is forced to break the fragile link between me
and my body that is constituted here by the word mine.
. . . Primary reflection is therefore forced to take up an
attitude of radical detachment. Secondary reflection does

not set out flatly to give the lie to these propositions; it manifests itself rather by a refusal to treat primary reflec- ion's separation of this body . . . from the self that I am, as final. Its fulcrum, or its springboard, is just that massive, indistinct sense of one's total existence which . . . we were trying . . . to locate as an existentialist centre" (pp. 90-92). This means that there is not only an immedi- ate awareness—whether of one's own existence, love, poverty, beauty or any other experience of life—nor a mere "first" abstract consideration of such, but that it is precisely the task of the philosopher to link this "first" consideration again with experience in the "second re- flection," which belongs to the concept of "mystery" in Marcel's sense. Only thus can a man come to grips with his own personality, which is not an "object" of thought, but an experienced subject, to be considered "exis- tentially" as a whole. This consideration also implies that all other persons cannot be thought of and consequently treated as "objects"; that man's relation to others is one of "intersubjectivity," which implies "availability" of one for another, affection and other personal relationships in which man "transcends" his own limitations and reaches the sphere of "being." But this communion of one finite being with other equally finite beings fails to satisfy man's thirst for absolute Being—and thus Marcel reaches God not by objective proof but through the discovery of his own need for a perfect, utterly unconditioned Thou.

In this outcome of his "reflections" on man's existence Marcel parts company with his fellow "existentialists." It is profoundly significant that the subtitle of one of his best-known books, *Homo Viator*, is "Introduction to a

Metaphysic of Hope." In it he lays his finger on the weak spot of non-Christian existentialism: "The merits of the work of Mr. Sartre, and not the least, consists . . . in showing clearly that a form of metaphysics which denies or refuses grace inevitably ends by setting up in front of us the image of an atrophied and contradictory world where the better part of ourselves is finally unable to recognise itself. It is . . . not enough to say that the world of Mr. Sartre does not seem to allow of any supernatural grafting, because the *pour-soi* has established itself there in a consciousness of its incompleteness which it even proudly claims as its privilege. Perhaps it should be added that the act by which the philosopher, be his name Nietzsche, Jaspers, or Sartre, shuts himself within the narrow circle of immanence, denying any other world or after life, appears in the last analysis much less as the expression of reason made wise by experience . . . than as the Luciferian refusal with which a rebellious individuality, intoxicated with itself, spurns the signs and calls to which Love alone could make it sensitive" (p. 183).

These are hard words, and a "traditional" philosopher might perhaps be forgiven if he objects that, his mind being differently constituted from that of Gabriel Marcel, the latter's way would not lead him to God either—that he requires the classic way of the Five Proofs to satisfy his need for logical argument. Nevertheless, Marcel has clearly seen the main weakness of atheist existentialism: that it fails to satisfy man's profound need for communion with his fellow creatures and his Creator, because it shuts him up in a meaningless universe where his only alternative to despair is an irrational determination to live *as if* existence had a meaning. On the other hand, as Newman had so clearly seen, men are not normally guided by merely rational considerations. And so Marcel, too, gives them something else: "Person—engagement—community—reality: there we have a chain of notions which do not readily follow from each other by deduction . . . but of which the union can be grasped by an act of the mind. . . . The ego, so long as it remains shut up within itself, that is to say the prisoner of its own feelings, of its covetous desires, and of that dull anxiety which works upon it, is really beyond the reach of evil as well as of good. It literally has not yet awakened to reality" (p. 22). It is Marcel's aim to deliver man from this prison in which he is confined by opening his mind to the possibility of communion, both with his fellow men and with God. For to him loneliness spells despair, whereas hope is bound up with communion: "In the first place hope is only possible on the level of the *us*, or we might say of the *agape*, and . . . it does not exist on the level of the solitary *ego*, self-hypnotized and concentrating exclusively on individual aims" (p. 10). So Marcel breaks through the fence that Kierkegaard had erected round the individual, shut up in his *Angst*, and places him once more in communion with his fellows, so that God need no longer be reached by wholly irrational "leaps" but is met in the communion of *agape*.

But he would not be a modern philosopher if *Angst* and despair played no part at all in his thought. "There is quite a general aspect," he writes, "under which human existence appears as a captivity and that, precisely when it takes on this form, it becomes so to speak subject to

hope. . . . By a paradox which need surprise only the very
superficial thinker, the less life is experienced as a captivity the less the soul will be able to see the shining
of that veiled, mysterious light, which . . . illumines the
very centre of hope's dwelling-place." (p. 32), and again:
"Despair is in a certain sense the consciousness of time
as closed or . . . of time as a prison—whilst hope appears
as piercing through time; everything happens as though
time, instead of hedging consciousness round, allowed
something to pass through it" (p. 53). It is difficult to
see how these passages could be interpreted except by
assuming that what Marcel here means by hope is the
theological virtue. Now any non-Christian philosopher as
well as a Thomist might object that this is an unwarranted
intrusion of theology into philosophy. And the reason for
this is that Marcel, too, is after all a pessimist *as far as
the natural sphere is concerned,* for he writes: "Do not let
us forget that . . . the general condition of man, even when
his life appears to be quite normal, is always that of a
captive, by reason of the enslavements of all kinds which
he is called upon to endure, if only on account of the
body, and more deeply still because of the night which
shrouds his beginning and end" (p. 58). Man as a captive
of his body. This is really the old Gnostic idea of the soul
imprisoned in matter; so Marcel can say: "It is precisely
the soul that is the traveler; it is of the soul and of the soul
alone that we can say with supreme truth that 'being'
necessarily means 'being on the way'" (p. 11).

So we see here, at the very heart of "Christian" existentialism the sudden reappearance of the age-old heresy
of Gnosticism, the *dualistic* form that *pessimism* took in

the first centuries of Christianity. The soul "imprisoned"
in the body, man held captive by his limitations, which
must be felt in all their rigor if "hope" is to arise—is this
really Christian philosophy? Is there not a subtle—I admit, a very subtle—failure to realize that man is a soul-in-
the-body, that he was created as such and redeemed as
such? That he is *Viator*, "on the way," both body *and*
soul? And that his captivity is due to sin, not to the body,
that the saints, even in captivity and under torture,
always felt themselves free: "If therefore, the son shall
make you free, you shall be free indeed"—free as human
beings, with—and despite—all the limitations of bodily
existence?

There is, as we shall see even more clearly in the following discussion of Catholic novelists and poets, a certain
unresolved tension between their life in a largely unbelieving world and their Christian faith. Christian hope
does precisely *not* spring from despair in a titanic, "And
yet!" It is the opposite of despair; it rests on the faith that
man and the world were created good and are capable of
once more becoming "good" through the Redemption.

On the other hand—and here we must own again that
it is very difficult to present Marcel's thought because
it does not seem to be quite consistent—he appears unduly optimistic when he writes: "If it is true that man's
trial is infinite in its varieties . . . it is no less certain that
by a symmetrical but inverted process, each one of us
can rise by his own special path from the humble forms of
communion which experience offers the most despised,
to a communion which is both more intimate and more
abundant, of which hope can be equally regarded as the

foreshadowing or the outcome" (p. 60). And "The believer is he who will meet with no insurmountable obstacle on his way towards transcendence" (p. 47). Here it may well be asked whether this does not imply that man can work out his own salvation independent of supernatural grace, merely by making good use of his experiences. And what exactly is "transcendence"? Is it merely transcending one's own ego by establishing communion with others? But why, then, is it only the "believer" who can achieve it!

All these questions will show that the marriage between Catholic and existentialist thought has so far not been a very happy one. It is supremely important for Catholic thinkers to take account of the most influential movements of non-Christian thought, but the way to a synthesis is full of pitfalls. After all, it needed an Augustine to christianize Plato and a Thomas Aquinas to do the same for Aristotle—and it should be noted that it is far more difficult to achieve such a synthesis for post-Christian thought, exactly because this contains a goodly number of distorted Christian elements, which cannot be "re-Christianized."

François Mauriac

If there is a fundamental residue of non-Christian pessimism in Marcel, this is even more so in the case of some widely acclaimed (and indeed very powerful and influential) Catholic authors.

In François Mauriac modern pessimism blends with the Jansenism that has been the bane of French Catholicism for centuries. Born in Bordeaux in 1885, he lost his father before he was two years old and was brought up, together with a sister and three brothers, by his devout, typically "bourgeois" mother. He was a pious boy, upon whom his First Communion made a profound impression, and who remained for a long time in the unquestioning faith of childhood, still expressed in his volume of verse, *Les Mains Jointes* (1909). Later, the temptations of life estranged him for a while from the sacramental life of the Church, though he never lost his faith. The tension between the demands of the faith and the desires of nature are at the very center of his work as a novelist. But it is a tension which is never resolved, and this, it seems to us, is due to the fact that for him grace does not perfect nature—as in Catholic teaching—but opposes it.

Mauriac's Jansenist upbringing expresses itself most forcefully in his attitude to sex. This fundamental human instinct is in the nature of things one of the main subjects of the novelist; and if his view of this is in any way distorted it will inevitably upset the balance of his work. Now, according to Christian teaching God made man in two sexes, and after he had created Adam and his wife He saw that, what He had made, was good. Mankind was to be propagated through the sexual act, which is good in itself but was vitiated through original sin insofar as its control by reason became very difficult. The Church consecrates it, as it were, through the Sacrament of Matrimony, which enables the spouses to keep it under control and to use it only for the procreation of children and as an expression of their mutual love. For in a properly balanced life the sexual union is the fully willed result of the love between man and woman, whose prototype according to St. Paul is nothing less than the union between Christ and His Church (Eph. 5:23ff.). Married love, which is the love of the whole man, whose sex is part of his divinely created being, is therefore a good thing, willed by God. It is, indeed, so exalted that it has become the accepted image through which the mystics of the Church express their love of God, and if men and women decide to remain unmarried for the love of God, this does not mean that they despise marriage, but, on the contrary, that they are prepared to sacrifice the most wonderful human relationship for the sake of something even higher than that, the total service of God.

Mauriac's view of sexual relations is truly terrifying, whether *Thérèse* (Desqueyroux) writes that desire transforms her husband into a monster (ch. 4), or Louis Pian, the narrator in *La Pharisienne* (ch. 11) says: "I believe that all the miseries of our human state come from our inability to remain chaste, and that men vowed to chastity would be spared most of the evils that weigh them down." Also, there is the frightful description of the wedding night of Jean Péloueyre in *A Kiss for the Leper*: "Long was the battle waged by Jean Péloueyre, at first with his own ice-bound senses, and then with the woman who was as one dead. As day was dawning a stifled groan marked the end of a struggle that had lasted six long hours. Soaked with sweat, Jean Péloueyre dared not make a movement. He lay there, looking more hideous than a worm beside the corpse it has at last abandoned."

These are only a few examples, but they are representative, especially if they be taken in combination with

his description of the physical appearances of his personages, who are almost always unattractive, if not
actually monsters of ugliness such as Jean Péloueyre and
Félicité Cazenave. The body is something horrid, and
more often than not houses an equally horrid mind. An
even moderately happy marriage is scarcely to be found
in Mauriac's novels except somewhere on the periphery,
such as that of Octavia and Monsieur Puybaraud in *La
Pharisienne*—but even this is cut short by the death of
Octavia during pregnancy, after which the widower
enters a Trappist monastery. And at the end of the book,
when Brigitte Pian, the "Pharisienne," finds a belated
happiness in the arms of her Calvinist doctor, Mauriac
cannot refrain from writing: "One dare not attempt to
visualize the squalid little efforts and contortions of those
bodies whose powers had not kept pace with the senti-
ments which stirred them" (ch. 16).

Thus Mauriac's characters start on their existence with
the scales, so to speak, heavily weighted against them
by the very fact that they are men and women and not
disembodied spirits. This situation is aggravated and
made actually hopeless by the fact that Mauriac deliberately refrains from showing the beauty of human
love and generosity in his work. In his Postscript to
Galigaï (*The Loved and the Unloved*) he discusses this
very reproach that has frequently been leveled against
him: "The social prejudices and priorities obtaining
among the 'insects' of a country society, would be matter
only for mockery and raillery, were it not for the fact that
there, as elsewhere, there, perhaps, more than elsewhere,
the secret drama of a sexual desire which is near neigh-

bour to disgust, finds its free development." And, a little further on: "I might well have called *The Loved and the Unloved*—Desire and Disgust. The subject of the book is one aspect of that hatred between the sexes which is rarely studied because, in the first place, it is something upon which we do not like to dwell, and because mutual love will always be a more pleasing spectacle to human beings so long as they continue to feel a need for love. I have not, in *The Loved and the Unloved*, deprived the reader of that spectacle." This passage is extraordinarily revealing and throws a good deal of light on the secret springs of Mauriac's work. Perhaps the most striking expression in it is the term "insects" for human beings. This is by no means a "slip of the pen." In *La Pharisienne* Mauriac thus describes a funeral congregation: "All these animal faces, with their ferrety noses, their foxy or rabbity masks and cow-like expressions," and the instances could be multiplied. With such descriptions Mauriac shows a contempt of his fellow humans, which is incompatible with his Christian faith, according to which they all are created in the image of God. It is this "image" which is so conspicuously absent from his personages, most of whom are really no more than "insects," greedy, malicious, obscene, and utterly loveless. They and their society, "the social prejudices and priorities . . . would be matter only for mockery and raillery" if they were not made utterly hideous by "the secret drama of a sexual desire." Mauriac hates the class prejudices which he depicts and which are certainly in many ways ridiculous, but again he forgets the "image" relationship—for surely they, too, are a reflection, however distorted and caricatured, of the hierarchical order of all being, and as such are not merely a matter "only for mockery and raillery."

It is perhaps in his apparent inability to see and reproduce this "image relationship" between God and man, between supernatural realities and their reflections in the realm of nature, that Mauriac's failure as a truly "Catholic" author is most apparent. For him there is God and supernature on the one side, and intrinsically vile and sinful nature on the other, and the two can be brought together only by what Mr. Jarret-Kerr very aptly calls a *gratia ex machina*.[3] In Mauriac's universe there is really no meeting point between God and man, which is precisely the image in which man was created; when grace comes it intrudes as a *gratia ex machina* into a world that is by rights closed to it. "The people I set out to paint are fallen creatures tainted from birth" says Mauriac in the Postscript cited above—but tainted in such a way that there is nothing left in them which has remained unsullied. This he admits himself: "The picture I have painted is indeed black. It shows mankind as warped, as showing to the world a mask fixed in a hard and hateful grimace. It shows humanity untouched by Grace."

Mauriac has been accused of painting an unreal world, and the truth of this accusation is borne out by this admission. For his persons do not live in a world untouched by grace. If he had described the life of a totally pagan society into which no missionary had ever penetrated this might be understandable—though even there God is capable of giving grace to men and women in good

---

[3] *François Mauriac*, Cambridge 1954, p. 46.

faith, though outside the sacraments of the Church. But
all Mauriac's personages are baptized Catholics who have
even made their First Communion, and many of them are
regular churchgoers. True, he shows their religion as
largely a formality, but how can he describe them as
"untouched by grace"? They may have abused grace,
failed to cooperate with it, but they cannot be said to be
"untouched" by it.

This attitude, of course, is due to Mauriac's fundamentally Jansenist outlook, however loudly he may protest against being charged with Jansenism. For him grace
is something special and extraordinary, not something
working—however invisibly—in and through the sacraments. But it is quite true, that the characters he creates
are untouched by grace; they—or at least the majority of
them—have no grace, neither in the theological nor even
in the popular sense of "natural grace." To give but a few
examples: He describes the relationship between the
possessive mother and her son in *Genetrix*: "There was
horror in the mute enmity that lay between Fernand and
his mother. . . . That he might not escape from her she had
willed that he should be a weakling. He saw his whole
life stretch before him arid, melancholy. . . . In the tangled
strands of the sticky web which his mother, for his protection, had set about him for half a century, he struggled
now, a great fat fly held captive" (ch. 9). Or, in *The
Knot of Vipers,* he describes a meeting between Louis,
the hero, and his former mistress: "Twenty years before
her nose had not been so big. In those days, too, her large
mouth had been adorned by a handsome set of teeth.
. . . But today her smile revealed a 'plate.' She must have

been walking fast, and the sour smell of her body battled successfully with the emanations from the marble-topped commode" (ch. 16).

When grace invades this world of evil-smelling human "insects" it finds nothing to meet it, as it were, halfway. Therefore the reader feels only too frequently somewhat embarrassed when it suddenly makes its appearance—for the *gratia ex machina* is just as unsatisfactory a device as the *deus ex machina*. *Genetrix* is a novel about a woman as hard as nails, possessed by an utterly selfish love for her son and eaten up with jealousy of her daughter-in-law, for whose death she is partly responsible, but who, from her grave, exercises an uncanny influence upon her son: "Only when it was hard upon the third hour was the sponge offered to the victim. How much more bitter than gall was the sight, upon that taut and suffering face, of so much love offered to another. Yet Félicité Czenave felt dimly that it was a good thing she should suffer for her son. What she did not know was that she had been crucified." Quite apart from the hideous comparison with the Passion of Christ, this suffering of a mother devoured by jealousy could hardly be said to have anything to do with Christian contrition. If it is meant to signify the intrusion of "grace" it surely is an "intrusion" in the real sense of the word, something entering unbidden from outside.

In *The Knot of Vipers* the advent of grace is better prepared, though it is all too obvious that the author is at great pains to point out the various stages of this preparation in the last pages of Louis' diary: "Something, as I sit to-night writing these lines, is stifling me, something

is making my heart feel as though it would burst—it is
the Love whose name at last I know, whose ador . . ."
Then death cuts short his confession. But the reader
could not have missed the point, for even before he starts
on his novel the author finds it necessary to tell us what
it is about: "The man here depicted was the enemy of his
own flesh and blood. His heart was eaten up by hatred
and by avarice. Yet, I would have you, in spite of his
baseness, feel pity, and be moved by his predicament.
All through his dreary life squalid passions stood between
him and that radiance which was so close that an oc-
casional ray could still break through to touch and burn
him: not only his own passions, but, primarily, those of
the lukewarm Christians who spied upon his actions, and
whom he himself tormented. Too many of us are similarly
at fault, driving the sinner to despair and blinding his
eyes to the light of truth. It was not money that this miser
really treasured. . . . What it was that he truly loved you
may discover who have the strength of mind, and the
courage, to follow his story to the end." It would have
been more convincing had Mauriac left us to discover this
for ourselves without all these signposts. But as his grace
is here, too, a *gratia ex machina,* it could not be seen
except by such unconvincing devices. For the miser with
hate in his heart remains so throughout the book—and
unless the author had told us beforehand that he did not
really treasure his money but something quite different,
the reader would have been unable to discover this by
his own unaided efforts.

In *A Woman of The Pharisees* the transformation of a
domineering "pious lady" whose ill-advised activities

bring misery to all with whom she comes into contact is more credible, though Brigitte Pian herself is a caricature as well as those feeble creatures who are quite incapable of standing up to her. This is really Mauriac's only novel in which the world is not painted entirely black, and even here there is missing one element, the importance of which most novelists, whether Christian or otherwise, have realized: the transforming power of a woman's love, whether for a man or for her children. This natural reflection of supernatural love is almost totally absent from his work; its place is taken, as he himself admits, by the "war of the sexes" and selfish possessiveness. Therefore grace cannot be shown to work in and through these human relationships, and it is significant that in one of his last novels, *Galigai* (1952), it makes its appearance only after the severance of human ties. For, as Mauriac says in his Postscript, "Galigai makes him (Nicolas) realize that the lusts of the flesh are productive of intense unhappiness, and that he has never really loved anyone but God."

But is this kind of love still Christian? St. John says in his First Epistle: "If any man say: I love God, and hateth his brother he is a liar. For he that loveth not his brother whom he seeth, how can he love God whom he seeth not?" (4, 20). This is the crux of the matter. For Mauriac the love of God is almost always divorced from the love of men, the First from the Second Commandment, though these are inseparable. "What I sought to express," he writes, "was precisely those shards and fragments of life as it is lived in a half-dead provincial town, and from which Nicolas separates himself at God's call." Yes, but the Christian's separation is a separation for love, not for hatred. Nicolas begins to love God only when he has learned to hate men—his former friend Gilles Salone as well as his mother, both of whom he now sees no longer as the idols he had once made of them, but with all their faults and insufficiencies.

"The unquenchable fires of hell are lit in this world and those whom theologians count as lost are marked for damnation at their birth and even before it" (*Les chemins de la mer*). This is a strange kind of theology, smacking more of Calvin and his double predestination than of Catholic doctrine. How is it that a Catholic writer can not only express himself thus but also give us the impression, in his work, that most of his personages really move in a hell of their own, without joy, without laughter, without the love that makes bearable the strain of life? We do not think that this is so, because, as Mauriac himself suggests somewhat conceitedly, "It may be that I was created . . . for the sole purpose of bearing witness to man's guilt when judged by the infinite innocence of God" (Postscript to *Galigai*). It may conceivably have also to do with his own temperament and with the trend of our time. We have seen before that this moves invariably in the direction of gloom and despair. It is only natural that for a Catholic this would translate itself into a pessimistic theological system such as exaggerated Augustinianism and its offspring Jansenism. But for an author to think himself created "for the sole purpose of bearing witness to man's guilt when judged by the infinite innocence of God" by means of best-selling novels is surely more than can be conceded to even the most orthodox writer, and, first of all, because he does not know at all how God judges, hence it is not for him to present man's guilt. An author who purposely creates bad characters and then sets himself up as their judge is a monstrosity. The fires of hell are not lit in this world but only in the next, and the novelist is certainly not there to light them in the world of fiction. But if a man thinks the very act by which God wishes mankind to propagate itself to be evil as Mauriac so obviously does, then hell begins, indeed, already on earth, because man's existence is poisoned at its source.

The picture he paints, shows "mankind as warped . . . a mask fixed in a hard and hateful grimace." But can this still be said to be the effect of sin? Indeed, are his personages, a Félicité Cazenave (*Genetrix*), a Louis (*Knot of Vipers*), a Madame Agathe (*The Loved and the Unloved*) really "sinners"—are they not much rather neurotics with more than a touch of the unreal and improbable about them? Sin can be confessed and forgiven, but the obsessions of the majority of Mauriac's figures belong by rights to the psychiatrist's consulting room. And like the obsessed, nearly all of them are wrapped up in themselves and their particular vices, whereas the community, whether it be the natural community of family and town or the supernatural one of the Church only exasperates them. In his *Journal*[4] Mauriac writes: "As soon as I set to work, everything takes on a color according to my eternal colors; even my most beautiful characters enter into a kind of sulphurous light which is natural to me and which I do not defend—for it is simply mine." Behind the work

---

[4] Cited in Jarrett-Kerr, p. 52.

of Mauriac is his hatred for the narrow, bigoted bourgeois and peasant world around Bordeaux where he grew up, and this hatred produces the "sulphurous light" and the "mask fixed in a hard grimace." But hatred is a bad counsellor, and so both the world as Mauriac paints it and the divine intrustions into it remain unconvincing.

Graham Greene

If hatred of the world he presents is characteristic of Mauriac, the same cannot be said of Graham Greene, though he has undergone Mauriac's influence. Besides, their types of religion are different, even if Jansenist leanings are not absent from Greene's work. But the Englishman is a convert, and, living in England, works in the midst of converts. For him the marvel of the Catholic "system," the wonder of the priesthood, of the Mass, of the miraculous element in Christianity is something wholly real; Catholicism is never, in his books, simply a convention of the bourgeoisie as it is in so many of Mauriac's works. And the world in which his persons move is not so much one of wickedness as of weakness. They are believers, but they are O so weak! Grace is there, the sacraments are there, but Greene's Catholics are quite incapable of cooperating with them. In fact the theology that seems at the root of his works is not so much Jansenism but Lutheranism, to put it quite crudely: the sinner remains a sinner despite his feeble efforts, but grace comes and covers it all up in the end.

As Graham Greene is a deliberately, one might almost

say self-consciously "Catholic" writer, it must be asked
what Catholicism means to his personages. There is a revealing passage in *The Heart of the Matter*. The hero,
Scobie, the police officer, has to search the cabinet of
a Portuguese captain where he finds concealed a letter to
his daughter in Germany which may or may not contain
a code message (the action takes place during the last
war). The captain entreats him not to send the letter to
the authorities, and in the course of the conversation
implies that Scobie, being an Englishman, is, of course a
Protestant. "I'm a Catholic, too, Scobie said. . . . He had
discovered suddenly how much they had in common: the
plaster statues with the sword in the bleeding heart: the
whisper behind the confessional curtains: the holy coats
and the liquefaction of blood: the dark side chapels and
the intricate movements, and somewhere behind it all the
love of God."

It does sound an odd agglomeration of features—
bleeding hearts, whisperings, dark chapels—but for the
saving words "and behind it all the love of God" it might
almost be the description of some pagan ritual. It is all
the external "trappings." And what exactly is the "love
of God" behind it? But to answer this question a closer
examination of Greene's novels is essential.

The field he covers is much wider than that of Mauriac;
he is a citizen of the British Commonwealth, a man who
has traveled widely, and whether he describes the streets
of London or of Hanoi, the roads in Mexico or the rains
of West Africa he does so with the insight and mastery of
the man who has penetrated their atmosphere and
learned their secret. But when it comes to the mystery of

Christianity, to the workings of grace in the human soul, his sight suddenly becomes dim. For he, too, is fundamentally pessimistic, perhaps even more so than Mauriac; human nature is corrupt and when grace comes to it it remains wholly outside.

The Power and the Glory has been widely acclaimed as his best novel from the Catholic point of view. It is the story of a very mediocre priest who remains behind in the Mexican state where the persecution is raging—not, it appears, from the overpowering love of God but through pride because another priest, his enemy, had fled. The hero, the "whisky priest" had been a very mediocre priest indeed, heartless and conceited; now in the persecution, when he himself falls into sin, the result of which is a child, he learns to have compassion with others: "How often the priest had heard the same confession—Man was so limited: he hadn't even the ingenuity to invent a new vice. . . . It was for this world that Christ had died: the more evil you saw and heard about you, the greater glory lay around the death; it was too easy to die for what was good and beautiful . . . it needed a God to die for the half-hearted and the corrupt." This is true, but God died for them not that they should stay half-hearted and corrupt, but that they should be reconciled to God and become saints. "Be ye perfect, as your heavenly Father is perfect." The moral theology of this priest is also very odd. "It sometimes seemed to him that venial sins— impatience, an unimportant lie, pride, a neglected opportunity—cut you off from grace more completely than the worst sins of all. Then, in his innocence, he had felt no love for anyone: now in his corruption he had learnt."

There are quite a number of very strange errors in this short passage. First of all, venial sins do not cut off a man from grace more completely than "the worst sins." But then the whisky priest considers pride a venial sin and the sins of the flesh "the worst sins of all." "Then, in his innocence"—that is before he had sinned with the woman Maria—but how can a man be "innocent" who had "felt no love for anyone"—whereas the two commandments in which all the Law and the prophets are summed up are those to love God and one's neighbor? Innocence does not consist merely in sexual abstinence—in fact there are nine other commandments beside the sixth and six other deadly sins beside lust, and in the days of his "innocence" the whisky priest had been guilty at least of pride and covetousness. But, and this is perhaps the most hideous trait in the novel, as soon as he has fled to a state where there is no persecution and is once more safe he falls back into all the habits of the days of his "innocence" and immediately starts haggling with the poor people about the price they are to pay for baptism: "He could feel the old life hardening round him like a habit, a stony case which held his head high and dictated the way he walked and even formed his words. . . . He said: 'What is it?' with his new-old manner of authority and impatience." If this is the way he behaves as soon as he is out of danger, he has learned nothing, and one can't help feeling that the communists of the novel are right to persecute such an utter travesty of Christianity. For the religion of the people to whom he goes back, too, has very little to do with the religion of Jesus, of St. John, and St. Paul, of a St. Teresa or a St. Vincent de Paul. They don't really want baptism and Holy Communion, as they will only be persecuted for it, and they don't really want the priest in their midst who endangers their lives; he realizes himself that for them he is "the trouble-maker whom for obscure and superstitious reasons they preferred not to betray to the police." For "superstitious reasons"—for these people are no real Christians, they consider the sacraments a kind of magic. And what of the priest's own religion, with his odd views about innocence and his simoniacal practices of charging high prices for the sacraments? The papers he kept sentimentally almost to the last were the cards on which he read "the words Altar Society, Guild of the Blessed Sacrament, Children of Mary." As he reflects on his life he says to himself: "I wasn't any use, but I stayed. At least, not much use. I'd got so that I didn't have a hundred communicants a month. If I'd gone I'd given God to twelve times that number. It's a mistake one makes." But is the usefulness of a priest's work to be counted by the number of his communicants? "We've always said the poor are blessed and the rich are going to find it hard to get into heaven. Why should we make it hard for the poor man too? [i.e. by bettering his lot] . . . It's better to let him die in dirt and wake in heaven. . . ." Our Lord certainly never told us to let the poor die in dirt, least of all did He expect His priests to act in such a way. "The Power and the Glory" —this means that the power and the glory of the priesthood shines forth even in a very unsatisfactory priest, that despite his sins and his meanness he gives God to the people. But does he really give Him? He administers the Sacraments, certainly—but are they not made ineffective by the very fact that both he and his people regard them as a kind of magic that is completely divorced from their moral life? "This place," he muses when he spends one night in prison, "was very like the world elsewhere: people snatched at causes of pleasure and pride in cramped and disagreeable surroundings: there was no time to do anything worth doing, and always one dreamed of escape." It is indeed a hopeless, "existentialist" world that Graham Greene depicts—and grace comes somewhere from outside and snatches you out of it.

It is the same in all his other novels. We have already cited the description of Catholicism in *The Heart of the Matter*. There Scobie is driven to suicide by his very religion. Graham Greene has a particular weakness for peculiar vows. In *The Heart of the Matter* Scobie has vowed on his wedding day "silently during the horrible little elegant ceremony among the lace and candles that he would at least always see to it that she [his wife Louise] was happy." It was in itself a crazy vow, and he was to find out only later that no human being can ensure another's happiness, but this did not prevent him from considering himself still bound by it. As he fails to get promoted, Louise is very unhappy in their oppressive little home in Sierra Leone and wants a holiday in South Africa, but for this he has to borrow money from Yusef, a shady Syrian dealer, and this involves him at once in some transactions not compatible with the duties of a police officer. While Louise is away he meets Helen, a nineteen-year-old widow who has survived forty days in the sea after the ship on which she and her husband were travelling had been torpedoed. This colorless young girl,

who is plain rather than pretty and to whom he is at-
tracted only by her pathetic situation, becomes his mistress. For in this way, he thinks, she will be saved not
only from Flight-Lieutenant Bagster, a young man much
given to drink, but also from returning to England, where
her life would be "The A.T.S. or the W.A.A.F., the blus-
tering sergeant with the big bust, the cookhouse and the
potato peelings, the Lesbian officer with the thin lips and
the tidy gold hair, and the men waiting on the Common
outside the camp"—but why adultery with the middle-
aged Scobie would be salvation as compared with these
other alternatives never becomes very clear. When
Louise, who has heard about her husband's association
with Helen, returns, the drama of the conflicting duties of
Scobie reaches its height. Louise wants him to go with
her to Holy Communion, for this would show that he
has given up his adulterous association with Helen.
Scobie finds this impossible because of his "duty" to
Helen: "Was it even love; or was it just a feeling of pity
and responsibility?" He goes to confession to Father
Rank, but he is yet another of Graham Greene's completely incompetent priests and is unable to help. As
Scobie refuses to avoid an occasion of being alone with
his mistress he is not given absolution, and so, in despair,
goes to Holy Communion in the state of mortal sin. Now
the strange thing—once more typical of Greene's presentation of Catholicism—is that Scobie does not really feel
remorse for his adultery, but he considers himself
damned if he goes to Holy Communion in the state of
mortal sin. The unbelieving Helen, to whom he confides
his dilemma, takes the common sense, and incidentally

the Catholic view, that if Scobie believes in hell as the punishment of mortal sin, he should not be together with her either. "To me that means—well, damnation. To take my God in mortal sin." Helen: "But I simply don't understand. If you believe in Hell, why are you with me now?" Scobie admits the logic: "You are right, of course: it ought to prevent all this. . . . And then, against all the teaching of the Church, one has the conviction that love —any kind of love—does deserve a bit of mercy. . . . I can regret the lies, the mess, the unhappiness, but if I were dying now I wouldn't know how to repent the love." Helen asks what difference it will make adding one more sin—going to Holy Communion in his state—to his other sins. He answers: "There is a difference—a big difference. . . . Now I'm just putting our love above—well, my safety. But the other—the other's really evil. . . . It's striking God when he's down—in my power."

This is a quite extraordinary argumentation. First of all, Scobie does not put their love above his own safety but above the law of God, which is a very different thing. The odd thing is that in this novel Graham Greene represents the saving of one's own soul as a somewhat selfish activity, as he also makes Scobie pray a little further on: "Make me put my own soul first." Whereas Christ Himself said: "What doth it profit a man, if he gain the whole world and suffer the loss of his own soul?" and St. Paul buffets his body, lest, having preached to others, he might himself be found wanting. Besides, it is an odd way of helping Helen to make her sin, too—as if the sixth commandment existed only for Catholics and for no one else. And what does Scobie—and Graham Greene—mean by

love? If Scobie really loved Helen he might surely find
other ways of helping her than committing adultery with
her, especially as, according to his own statement, he is
not actually passionately in love with her. But, what is
stranger still, it is not the adultery that worries Scobie,
but going to Holy Communion in mortal sin, which he
seems to think is an unforgivable sin for "It's striking
God when he's down—in my power." But God is never
really in man's power. Even in Holy Communion God is
not "helpless," a voluntary prisoner given up to man's
whims. Christ remains as impassible, that is as incapable
of suffering, in the Blessed Sacrament as He is at the right
hand of the Father in heaven. We cannot hurt *Him* by re-
ceiving Him unworthily—we can only hurt ourselves.
And if a man has consciously received Holy Communion
in the state of mortal sin it certainly makes the former sin
worse—but the sacrilege, too, can be forgiven in the same
way as the adultery. Scobie, however, is convinced that
he is "damned for all eternity—unless a miracle happens.
. . . What I've done is far worse than murder—that's an
act, a blow, a stab, a shot: it's over and done, but I'm
carrying corruption around with me. . . . Never pretend I
haven't shown my love."

The Heart of the Matter has often been acclaimed as a
great Catholic novel. But the religion presented in it is
Catholic only in its trappings. As in Lutheranism, the sinner is quite incapable of freeing himself from his sin,
which drives him even to suicide. And then the epitaph.
Father Rank, the ineffectual priest says: "I think, from
what I saw of him, that he really loved God." His wife:
"He certainly loved no one else." "And you may be in the

right of it there, too," Father Rank replied. It is the same view of the love of God we have met in Mauriac, when he writes in his Postscript to *Galigai* that she makes Nicolas realize "that the lusts of the flesh are productive of intense unhappiness, and that he has never really loved anyone but God." But in Graham Greene's novel this love of God has an even stranger way of expressing itself —for Christ said: "If you love me, keep my commandments"—it is a false love, a false "pity"—the principal emotion analyzed in the novel—which shows itself by breaking them.

In *The End of the Affair* the novelist attempts to present the conversion of a sinner. The principal figure of the book is Sarah Miles, the unfaithful wife of a civil servant, who after many minor "affairs" falls seriously in love with Bendrix, a moderately successful novelist. He tortures both of them with his jealousy, and their love, too, in an exclusively sensual affair—at least there is nothing in the novel to suggest anything else. The background is provided by London during the air-raids, and in one of these, when Sarah and Bendrix have just been "making love" in his flat, he goes down to see whether it is possible for them to shelter in the basement. Just then there is an explosion, the front door is blown in and he is buried beneath it. When he fails to come back to her, Sarah goes down to investigate. "I didn't see Maurice at first, and then I saw his arm coming out from under the door. I touched his hand: I could have sworn it was a dead hand. ... I knelt down on the floor ... Maurice was dead. Dear God, I said. ... Make me believe. ... Let him be alive and I *will* believe. ... I love him and I'll do anything if you'll make him alive. I said very slowly, I'll give him up for ever, only let him be alive with a chance. . . . And then he came in at the door, and he was alive, and I thought now the agony of being without him starts, and I wished he was safely back dead again under the door."

We are given to understand that this was a real miracle in response to the prayer of the till then unbelieving Sarah. Now this is in itself highly improbable, to say the least. Miracles are very few and far between, and none more so than the miracle of bringing a dead man back to life. But, what is even more important in this context, God does not do a miracle in answer to a kind of ultimatum put to Him: You bring that person back to life and I will believe and not commit any more adultery with him. We have Christ's own words for it: "An evil and adulterous generation seeketh a sign: and a sign shall not be given it."

However, after this tremendous miracle Sarah tries to keep away from Bendrix. Not that she now becomes a faithful wife, on the contrary, she is at first so shaken that she tries some other men, telling herself that, after all, she has only promised to give up Bendrix, not anyone else. However, she finds that she has lost all taste for others and finally succumbs to the temptation of seeing Bendrix again—the meeting stirs up all her passion for him and only a violent coughing fit at the right moment prevents her from beginning all over again. Shortly after that he follows her into a church where she has sought refuge from him; again she almost yields—before the very altar, but feels too ill to stay and goes home. Within a week she is dead—but not before having written him a last letter in which she says "I don't want to live without you, and I know one day I shall meet you on the Common and then I won't care a damn about Henry [her husband] or God or anything. But what's the good, Maurice? I believe there's a God—I believe the whole bag of tricks, there's nothing I don't believe, they could subdivide the Trinity into a dozen parts and I'd believe. They could dig up records that proved Christ had been invented by Pilate to get himself promoted and I'd believe just the same. I've caught belief like a disease."

So, first of all, she had not been morally converted at all—she knows she would become her former lover's mistress again if the opportunity offered. But what kind of a faith is this that she has "caught like a disease"? It is a faith that knows no reason, that even knows no truth, for it actually visualizes the possibility of a cogent proof of the absurdity of her belief. But the faith of the Church rests on the historically attested truth of the Resurrection; it is a faith worthy of rational human beings; indeed, you need grace to accept it, but you do not "catch" it like a disease. Then, after her death, it comes out that her mother, a Catholic who had married outside the Church, actually had her baptized when she was two years old while on holiday in France, though Sarah herself knew nothing about it. "I always had a wish that it would 'take.' Like vaccination," says the mother. First "a disease," now "vaccination." And so it did "take" at the end, for Sarah had put herself under instruction shortly before her death.

But this is not the end of the strange events in this novel. For after her death Sarah actually begins to work

miracles—she cures a child of appendicitis and a free
thinker of a disfiguring birth mark. Bendrix comments:
"If this God exists, I thought, and if even you—with your
lusts and your adulteries and the timid lies you used to
tell—can change like this, we could all be saints by leaping as you leapt, by shutting the eyes and leaping once
and for all: if *you* are a saint, it's not so difficult to be a
saint. It's something He can demand of any of us, leap."
And so, surprisingly enough, we are back at the beginning
of this book: we are back at Kierkegaard and his "leap."

No, indeed, if Sarah Miles were a saint, sanctity would
not be difficult. But men do not "leap" into sanctity, as
little as they catch faith "like a disease." Grace works
both much less conspicuously and much more effectively.
It transforms the very will of a person, so that he becomes
capable of keeping out of sin and turns his back on his
former life. But Sarah Miles does nothing of the kind: "I
just want him like I used to in the old days . . . I want to
be drinking with him in a bar . . . I want ordinary corrupt
human love." And each time this "corrupt" love is made
impossible not by her own will, but by some unexpected
external intervention. As she herself confesses: "I've done
my best to break it [the vow she made during the air
raid], but it didn't work." Yet God respects the free will
of His creatures—He does not intervene forcibly each
time temptation presents itself. Then conversion and
sanctity would indeed be easy—we need only take the
"leap" into belief and all would be supernaturally ar-
ranged for us (?).

"I want ordinary corrupt human love." But is ordinary
human love necessarily corrupt? Graham Greene is as

incapable as Mauriac of presenting a true love between man and woman, a love that elevates and fulfills, because for him, too, sex is something sordid, and he can see woman only as the mistress, never as the wife (except as a nagging one like Louise Scobie) and mother. "Wouldn't we all do better not trying to understand, accepting the fact that no human being will ever understand another, not a wife a husband, a lover a mistress, nor a parent a child? Perhaps that's why men have invented God—a being capable of understanding. Perhaps if I wanted to understand I would bamboozle myself into belief." Thus says Fowler, the disillusioned journalist in *The Quiet American*. And sometimes it seems as if this were really the underlying philosophy of its author. The almost desperate clinging to the miraculous element in Catholicism—so obvious also in *The Potting Shed*—combined with a preoccupation with the seamy side of human life, with suicide, adultery, drink, and the rest, make it seem as if faith were truly something imported from outside, and God—this God who is the only one who "understands" Pinkie, the whisky priest, Scobie, Sarah Miles, and all the other broken men and women of Graham Greene's novels—were but the creature of a faith that must needs take the Kierkegaardian "leap" in order to escape from the despair that is forever threatening human existence.

5

POETS OF CHRISTIAN HOPE

Paul Claudel

IN THE preceding pages we have been trying to analyze some manifestations of contemporary gloom, the refusal to believe in the original goodness even of this world, in the efficacy of grace that can transform the human soul, and, above all, in the power of love. For the "love" shown by Sartre and Françoise Sagan, Mauriac and Greene is not love—it is but the sexual urge, divorced from the great spiritual reality which gives it its meaning. There is no sign in all the writers so far discussed that full human love—in which sex must also play its part, for God created man male and female—is nothing degrading, but, on the contrary, elevates the human being. Certainly, even human love must finally be transcended, for in heaven there will be no marriage. Nevertheless, the love between man and woman is the earthly image of the love between Christ and the Church; and if the priests and religious of the Church sacrifice human love in order to give themselves wholly to God, they do so not because marriage is something vile—as Graham Greene for example says in *Brighton Rock*—but because it is the greatest human good they can offer God.

Paul Claudel is a lonely figure in modern literature. Unlike Mauriac his countryman, but like Graham Greene, he has traveled widely, and his diplomatic career took him to the Far East as well as to the United States. But his conception of the world is totally different from theirs. His very birthday—August 6, which is the Feast of the Transfiguration—seems to be an omen: for to him the whole world is transfigured by the grace of Christ, and sin itself is not outside the scope of divine Providence. It is well known that he lost the faith of his baptism as a youth under the impact Voltaire and Renan made on his impressionable mind, but he was converted on Christmas Day, 1886, when he heard Mass, and later Vespers, at Notre Dame in Paris. He finally made his confession four years later at Christmas 1890, being thus restored to the full sacramental communion of the Church. From then onward the peace and joy of a fully lived Christian life expressed itself in a series of poems, dramatic works, and later also spiritual writings. But if we say "peace and joy" this must not be mistaken for easy optimism. Claudel knows the power of sin as well as Mauriac and Greene, but he knows the real power of grace, the innate nobility of human nature better than they, and he is not afraid to confess them. Neither is he afraid to depict adultery— but how differently from the English author!

Partage de Midi (1906) is Claudel's version of the "war of the sexes," and of the sinful union between a man and a married woman. Ysé is the woman between three men, her husband, de Ciz, Amalric, who has once been in love with her, and Mesa, who wanted to be a priest but was refused and is still longing for the perfect spiritual fulfilment that had been denied him. He and Ysé realize very soon that they were "made for each other"; Mesa tries to resist the attraction, but Ysé, to whom he admits that he has never had a woman, tempts him, and during the prolonged absence of her husband she becomes his mistress.

But she comes to understand very soon that she cannot fulfill his most intimate longing, that he remains a stranger in her arms, that there is something in him that does not belong to her. The only solution for her is to leave him. Being with child, she flees to Amalric, but finally rejoins Mesa in a violent death during a siege, when their love is consummated in sacrifice, and Mesa is purified, *"le grand mâle dans la gloire de Dieu."*

The love between Ysé and Mesa, sinful though it is, has yet the redemptive power that is a quality of all true love: it changes both. At the end of the play Mesa is no longer the frustrated young man of the first scenes, the *"sacré petit bourgeois"* as Ysé once called him, nor is Ysé still the coquette who likes to play with men. They have passed through a fire of adulterous love, but have been purified by the suffering it has brought to both of them.

More than twenty years later Claudel resumed the same theme in what is perhaps his greatest drama, *Le Soulier de Satin* (1928-9). Here again a man loves a married woman, but this time the action is concerned not only with the mutual relations of four characters, but takes place in the vast setting of history, ranging over a century and four continents. The characters that take

part in the tremendous play are not confined only to the
human sphere; the guardian angel, the moon and even
the "double shadow" of a man and a woman take part
in it. The time is the sixteenth century, and the love between Don Rodrigue and Dona Prouhèze, two full-
blooded personalities of the Renaissance, is played out
within the tumultuous events of the age that followed the
discovery of America and the Reformation of Luther. It is
an age when the ordered little world of the Middle Ages
has broken up and all is in ferment, when individual men
are as violent as the great events around them. But over
this new, seething world of the coming age Divine Providence watches, too, and sin and sanctity are intertwined.
In the opening scene of the play a Jesuit missionary,
bound to the mast of a sinking ship as Christ was nailed
to the Cross, prays for his brother, Rodrigue, who had
abandoned a religious vocation to become an adventurer
and conqueror: "But, Lord, it is not so easy to escape
from You, and if he does not go to you by the way of
light, may he go by that which is dark; and if not directly,
may he go there indirectly. . . . And if he desires disorder,
may it be a disorder that involves the shaking and
splitting of the walls around him which prevent his salvation. . . ." And Dona Prouhèze, a woman made for passion
and adventure but married to a much older, unexciting
husband (Don Pélage), prays too: "Virgin Mother, I
give you my slipper. Virgin Mother, keep my unhappy
little foot in your hand. I warn you that presently I shall
not see you any more and that I shall turn everything
against you. But when I shall try to rush into evil, may it
be with a limping foot." And so the great drama of pas-

sionate love becomes also a drama of renunciation. Only twice do the lovers see each other. At the end of the Second Day Prouhèze tells Rodrigue that she will stay at Mogador, where her husband has sent her as governor of the castle, which is actually held by Don Camille, he, too, a typical adventurer of the time, who is in love with her. Don Rodrigue leaves and goes to America where the King of Spain has ordered him to govern, and the Guardian Angel explains to Prouhèze the meaning of their love and of her sacrifice. "For some," he says, "the intellect suffices. That is the spirit which speaks purely to the spirit. But for the others the flesh, too, must gradually be evangelized and converted. And which flesh is more powerful to speak to man than the flesh of woman? Now he can no longer desire you without desiring at the same time where you are." For Prouhèze's husband has died and she is now married to Don Camille, since Rodrigue, whom she called back, did not receive her letter. And so, still irrevocably separated from him she is fulfilling her vocation, to draw her lover to God. For, like Mesa in *Partage de Midi,* he, too, really desires something from her which no earthly woman can give, but to the possession of which she can lead him. So Prouhèze tells him: "Accuse but yourself, Rodrigue. What no woman was able to give, why demand it from me? . . . And later, when Don Pélage had died and I sent you that call, Yes, perhaps it was better that it did not reach you. I should have been only a woman soon to die on your heart, and not this eternal star for which you thirst. . . . Renounce yourself. Throw all away. Give all, that you may receive all!" And so Rodrigue at last gives her up forever, but she leaves him the child of her marriage with Don Camille, which is mystically the child of her love for Rodrigue and who, in the Fourth Day, appears as Dona Sept-Épées.

The historical background of this last part of the play is the defeat of the Armada. Don Rodrigue is now an old man who employs a Japanese to paint pictures of the saints according to his specifications. But the false news that the Armada has landed in England and that this country will be given to Rodrigue to govern, once more rouses his old spirit of adventure. The king who mocks him causes an actress to play Mary Queen of Scots to him, to whom he is to restore England. He consents, and this illusion becomes in his mind part of a gigantic plan to bring the whole world into the Catholic Church. But Sept-Épées knows that this is only a dream, that God works in a different way, that the humble limited works of charity are more pleasing to Him than the spectacular deeds which Rodrigue desires. For the Armada has been destroyed and on the order of the King Rodrigue has been captured and is to be sold as a slave. In the last scene he is in chains between soldiers in the company of Friar Léon, who had once married Prouhèze to Don Camille. When Rodrigue hears this, his old love flares up once more. But at the words of the Friar he comprehends that now at last he is freed from all earthly love and ambitions. At this moment an old Carmelite Sister appears begging for alms, and the Friar persuades her to take Rodrigue, who will henceforth live as a servant "in the shadow of Mother Teresa." The play ends on a triumphal note, when Friar Léon cries out: "Deliverance to the souls held captive."

The love of Prouhèze has finally brought Rodrigue
salvation, even though it was a forbidden love, for to
those whom God loves all things work together for their
good, *"Etiam peccata"*—even the sins, according to the
motto of the book, taken from St. Augustine. The love of
Prouhèze has become a means of salvation, but only because it was a sacrificial love that was never consummated. For, as Claudel says in *Partage de Midi:* "Woman
is a promise that cannot be kept"—the deepest aspirations
of man's soul that tend towards the Infinite cannot be
fulfilled by human love. But because the love between
Rodrigue and Prouhèze leaves both of them deeply
wounded it can lead them to God, and it is for woman, to
whom sacrifice and renunciation comes more easily than
to man, to show him the way.

Woman as a victim of love, this theme recurs again and
again in Claudel's works, in its purest and most beautiful
form in the lovely "mystery play" *L'annonce faite à Marie.*
Like the *Soulier de Satin, L'annonce,* too, has an historical background, but here it plays a less important part
than in the larger work. It is the time of Jeanne D'Arc,
the Antipopes and the building of the great Gothic ca-
thedrals—here as in *Le Soulier,* Claudel is not concerned
with chronological exactitude but with the spirit of the
age—the latter age of "Catholic Europe," in which the
fissures that were to widen into the great ruptures were
already noticeable.

Pierre de Craon, the patient builder of churches, who
once passionately desired the pure young girl Violaine,
who rejected him, comes back, a leper, asking for con-
tributions to his new church. While he speaks to Violaine,

the Angelus rings, and they sing it together. She then gives him the engagement ring which Jacques Hury, her fiancé, had given to her, but Pierre demands more. He tells her that she is the cause of his leprosy—a disease traditionally associated with the sin of impurity—"It is you who have brought this evil upon me by your beauty, for before I had seen you, I was pure and happy." But she is happy in her love for Jacques: "I am Violaine, I am eighteen years old . . . my fiancé is called Jacques. . . . All is perfectly clear. . . . Ah, how beautiful this world is and how happy I am!" Pierre tells her that sanctity consists not in being stoned by the Turks, but "in doing the commandment of God at once, whether this means to remain in our place or to ascend higher"—and he makes it clear that her vocation is not to become the wife of Jacques but to "ascend higher." As he says goodbye to her, she kisses him in a sudden emotion of intense pity with his unhappiness, as she will explain later: "The poor man was a leper, and I was so happy on that day."

But Mara, her wicked sister, herself in love with Jacques Hury, has seen this kiss and interprets it quite wrongly. She persuades her mother to tell Violaine that she, Mara, ought to marry him, and she tells Jacques that Violaine has deceived him with Pierre de Craon which he does not at first believe. Then follows the great scene between Violaine and Jacques in which she declares her deep love for him and makes him promise that he, too, will love her forever. After that she shows him the spot on her body where the leprosy has just attained her. At once his attitude to her is changed completely. He believes what Mara has told him, tells Violaine that she is damned and a daughter of the devil; "This is the great love you had for me?" she asks, and refuses to defend herself by telling him the truth. For her mother has told her that Mara has threatened to kill herself if Jacques were not to marry her—and as Jacques, the poor mediocre man who Pierre de Craon realized intuitively was not worthy of her, has failed her completely, she sacrifices her love for the sake of her sister's salvation and goes out into the woods to live as a leper, far from all human society, alone with God.

Eight years intervene between this and the third act. On Christmas Eve, Mara, who has married Jacques, comes to find Violaine, demanding from her that she bring her baby girl who is dead, back to life. Violaine, who is now also blind, is terrified: "Ask of me to recreate heaven and earth!" Mara: "But it is written that you can breathe on this mountain and throw it into the sea." "I can, if I am a saint." "You must be a saint if a miserable woman supplicates you." "Ah, supreme temptation! I swear, I declare, I protest before God that I am not a saint." "Give me back my child!" Then the bells begin to ring and Violaine asks Mara to read to her the Office of Christmas, while the sound of the bells of the Midnight Mass mingle with the trumpets announcing that Jeanne D'Arc brings the King to Rheims for his coronation. At Violaine's bidding Mara continues to read the Office and angelic choirs sing the responses. Suddenly Violaine cries out. The dead child that Mara has laid into her arms has come to life, but her eyes that were black like Mara's have become blue like Violaine's.

In the last act Pierre de Craon appears once more, the dying Violaine in his arms.* She has been attacked by Mara, who is still jealous of her, because she knows that Jacques has never loved her as he had loved Violaine. Pierre leaves her with Jacques, and now at last she tells him that she has never deceived him: "If you had believed in me, who knows if you might not have healed me?" Yet all has been for the best: "Now that I am wholly broken the perfume is exhaled. And you believe all, simply because I have laid my hand on your head." The play ends as it has begun, with the sound of the Angelus, followed by the communion bell; "The three notes, like an ineffable sacrifice, are gathered in the heart of the sinless Virgin," says Pierre de Craon, whose leprosy has been healed and "Violaine the leper is in glory, Violaine the blind in the sight of all."

Again the love of a woman is an agent of redemption; but this time it is the utterly pure, selfless love of a girl who sacrifices herself for the salvation of her sister. Mara —"the bitter one"—is the epitome of selfishness, the personified refusal of submission to the will of God; Violaine is all acceptance, and by accepting the most cruel sacrifice and forgiving all, even her sister who has murdered her, she becomes the instrument of redemption for many.

In this play, as in Graham Greene's *The End of the Affair* and *The Potting Shed*, a miracle of resurrecting a dead person is at the center of the action. But how differ-

* The citations from *L'announce faite à Marie* are made from the original edition. Recent stage versions have some changes in dramatic action and dialog.—[Editor]

ent is the whole atmosphere in which it takes place! In both cases described by Graham Greene, the miracle is, as it were, God's part in a bargain. In the *End of the Affair* Sarah offers to believe in God and to give up her adulterous liaison in exchange for her lover's life; in *The Potting Shed* Father William Callifer offers his faith in exchange for the life of his nephew. It has been noted before that the whole idea of obtaining a miracle in exchange for something one offers to God is foreign to the Christian conception of miracles, which are gratuitous graces God may grant to humble prayer, not divine acts performed in exchange for some human gift (least of all the gift of one's very faith). The miracles in Graham Greene's works savor suspiciously of a kind of Catholic bravado (see, you unbelievers, how we Catholics believe in miracles and how they happen to us as soon as we ask for them!).

But this is not the way in which they happen in reality. Violaine, the woman who has offered herself as a victim for the salvation of others, who has accepted the most atrocious suffering with perfect love and resignation, might indeed count upon her power of intercession to ask for a miracle. But she recoils in terror from such a presumption: "I am not a saint"—for only saints can work miracles, and even they only with fear and trembling. Breaking the laws that God has given to nature is a rare and exceptional thing—even at Lourdes miracles happen very seldom—and it needs sanctity to obtain them. The miracle of *L'annonce faite à Marie* is a sign of Violaine's sanctity; more, it is a sign of the new life that Christ has brought us, a fitting climax of the liturgy of the Holy

Night of Christmas, whereas the raisings of the dead in Graham Greene's work take place in an atmosphere of adultery and suicide, *miracula ex machina,* which strain credulity to the breaking point.

For the world of Claudel is a coherent world, just as Catholic Christianity is a coherent faith. God is the supreme Ruler of the universe He has created; He works in the minds of men as much as in the events of history and in the rare miracle His saints are allowed to perform. The stars and the angels are in His hands, the souls of sinners and of the innocent, and sin itself—sinful love above all—is, as it were, the fautly raw material from which His omnipotence can yet fashion salvation. For, in contrast to so many contemporary writers who seem to be not only fascinated but actually hypnotized by the seamy side of life, by everthing that is sordid and seedy in the human character and human love, Claudel sees the divine spark in man, that indestructible image in which he was created and through which God has, as it were, a hold on him and can raise him up even from the depth of sin and revolt. For Claudel the whole world reflects not only the suffering of the Cross but the glory of the Resurrection. In his book of Meditations, *A Poet Before the Cross* he writes: "All creation visible and invisible, all history, all the past, all the present and all the future, all nature, all the treasure of the saints multiplied by grace—all that is at our disposal, all that is our prolongation and our prodigious equipment. All the saints and all the angels are ours. We can use the intelligence of Saint Thomas, the arm of Saint Michael, the heart of

Joan of Arc and of Catherine of Siena. We have only to
touch all the latent resources in us to see them rise up.
All that is good and important and beautiful from one end
of the earth to the other, all that creates holiness in the
world, is, in a sense, our work." For Claudel is truly the
poet of the Mystical Body, whether in *L'Otage* Sygne
de Coûfontaine sacrifices her honor to save the Pope and
the Church, in *Le Soulier de Satin* the prayers of the
Jesuit priest finally guide his brother Rodrigue to salvation, or the sufferings of Violaine bring peace to her
family.

Claudel's poetic dramas offer a truly Christian interpretation of the world. But none of them is actually a
"play" in the accepted sense of the word, and all of them
might bear the sub-title "*Mystère*" which Claudel gives
to *L'annonce faite à Marie*, for they are all "mysteries,"
and their persons and actions have a tremendous sym-
bolic significance that tends to endanger their human
reality. For they are more than once on the point of
ceasing to be human beings and becoming mere symbols,
identified with what the poet wants to express through
them but without an independent life of their own. This
is perhaps also the reason why they give a peculiarly
timeless impression: the twentieth century is almost absent from Claudel's work, except perhaps in a few passages in *Partage de Midi*, which is the reflection of a personal experience. The French diplomat who has been
involved in politics for about half a century situates his
religious drama in a sphere far removed from our everyday world—which gives it its peculiar poignancy but also
a certain lack of relation to contemporary problems.

T. S. *Eliot*

The work of Thomas Stearns Eliot is closer to us, though it, too, is saturated with symbolism. Eliot is not a Catholic. Born in St. Louis, Missouri, he was brought up in the Congregationalist tradition of his homeland, which is responsible for the moral integrity and purpose of his outlook. Educated at Harvard, the Sorbonne, and Oxford, the European tradition made a profound impact on his mind; at the same time the purposelessness and degradation of a society that had lost its moral and religious bearings affected him deeply. At the age when Claudel had found his faith in the fullness of the Catholic Church, Eliot became an agnostic, and his bewilderment —and the bewilderment of a whole generation—is reflected in his early volumes of verse, *Prufrock* and the *Poems* of 1920, reaching its climax in *The Waste Land* (1922) and *The Hollow Men* (1925). In his longing for a way out of the moral and religious impasse, Eliot seizes upon the symbolism of the fertility cults and the Grail legend as opposed to the barrenness of a society that has degraded human love and marriage to a sexual exercise devoid alike of mutual surrender and the healthy desire to make it fruitful in the child. All that is left to the world of the modern city is a tradition gone dead: "Daguerrotypes and Silhouettes, / Her grandfather and great great aunts, / Supported on the mantel piece / *An Invitation to the Dance*" (*A Cooking Egg*), and the human beings that people it are in a permanent state of indecision incapable of good and evil alike: ". . . time yet for a hundred indecisions, / And for a hundred visions and revisions, / Before the taking of a toast and tea. . . . / Do I dare / Disturb the universe? / In a minute there is time / For decisions and revisions which a minute will reverse. . . . I have measured out my life with coffee spoons. . . ." This indecision is not that of Hamlet, it is something at the same time far more trivial and far more insidious: "No! I am not Prince Hamlet, nor was meant to be; / Am an attendant lord. . . . / Deferential, glad to be of use, / Politic, cautious, and meticulous; / Full of high sentence, but a bit obtuse. . . . / Shall I part my hair behind? / Do I dare to eat a peach?" and then, the greatest bliss open to Prufrock and his likes: "I shall wear white flannel trousers, and walk upon the beach" only to be followed by harsh disappointment: "I have heard the mermaids singing, each to each. / I do not think that they will sing to me."

In *The Waste Land* this empty, meaningless world— incidentally the very world of Graham Greene's novels —is seen in all its horror. It is the land of the Fisherking of the Grail legend who has lost his virility and whose country has therefore become barren: "I sat upon the shore / Fishing, with the arid plain behind me / Shall I at least set my lands in order?" The "Unreal City" that has lost its roots; "For you know only / A heap of broken images." One after the other rootless people of this country appear, who call April "the cruellest month," because it stirs "Dull roots with spring rain" and brings new life which they resent, for they themselves are "neither living nor dead." In section II, "A Game of Chess," this sterility is typified in the bored love-making of the "upper classes": "What shall we ever do? / The hot water at ten. / And if it rains, a closed car at four. / And we shall play a game of chess, / Pressing lidless eyes and waiting for a knock upon the door" and the fear of children that has penetrated even into the "lower" strata of society: "You *are* a proper fool, I said. / Well, if Albert won't leave you alone, there it is, I said, / What you get married for if you don't want children?"

And after this the "love-making" itself in Part III: "The typist home at teatime, clears her breakfast, lights / Her stove, and lays out food in tins. . . . / He, the young man carbuncular, arrives, / A small house agent's clerk, with one bold stare . . . / The time is now propitious, as he guesses, / The meal is ended, she is bored and tired, / Endeavours to engage her in caresses / Which still are unreproved, if undesired. . . . / His vanity requires no response, / And makes a welcome of indifference. . . . / Bestows one final patronising kiss, And gropes his way, finding the stairs unlit . . . / She turns and looks a moment in the glass, / Hardly aware of her departed lover; / Her brain allows one half-formed thought to pass: / 'Well now that's done: and I'm glad it's over.' " The act designed to propagate mankind could not be debased further—even passion is totally absent from it—and the stairs are "unlit." All has become meaningless: "On Margate Sands; / I can connect / Nothing with nothing."

The total absurdity and arid drought of this world—which is also the world of Kafka and Sartre and Camus and Anouilh—can be healed only by death, the "Death by Water," which is the title of Part IV, and which probably signifies not only the ritual use of water in the mystery religions but also in baptism; for already at the end of Part III Eliot had referred to St. Augustine "To Carthage then I came," and "O Lord Thou pluckest me out," and also to Buddha: "Burning burning burning burning." As the author himself points out in his notes, "the collocation of these two representatives of eastern and western asceticism . . . is not an accident." And so in the last part (Part V) of the poem the general disease is, indeed, once more shown up in all its fearsomeness: "Dead mountain mouth of carious teeth that cannot spit / Here one can neither stand nor lie nor sit" but the cure is also hinted, not yet, it is true, in fully Christian terms, but with some words of the Upanishads: "Datta, dayadhvam, damyata," Give, sympathize, control: "The awful daring of a moment's surrender / Which an age of prudence can never retract . . . / We think of the key, each in his prison . . . / The boat responded gaily, to the hand expert with sail and oar / . . . your heart would have responded / Gaily, when invited, beating obedient / To controlling hands."

The hope of the redemption even of this empty, arid world of modern men is given a more definitely Christian form in "The Hollow Men"—the last of the poems describing the "Waste Land" of contemporary civilization. "We are the hollow men / We are the stuffed men / Leaning together / Headpiece filled with straw. . . . / Remember us—if at all—not as lost / Violent souls, but only / As the hollow men / The stuffed men." The "lost violent souls" have at least a certain grandeur—but these, "the hollow men, the stuffed men" have not even that. They correspond to the "lukewarm" who, because they were neither cold nor hot will be vomited out of the mouth of

Christ (Apoc. 3:16). For "this is the dead land / This is cactus land" from which "the eyes" are absent. Whose eyes? "In this last of meeting places / We grope together / And avoid speech. . . . / Sightless, unless / The eyes reappear / As the perpetual star / Multifoliate rose / Of death's twilight kingdom / The hope only / Of empty men." The combination of the star, the rose and the hope, all Marian images (morning star, mystical rose, our hope) strongly suggest that the eyes are Our Lady's, and the reference is probably to the *Salve Regina:* "Turn . . . thine eyes of mercy towards us."

The last section of the poem is the final expression of the struggle between the deepest aspirations of the human being and the selfish attachments that prevent their fulfilment: "Between the idea / And the reality / Between the motion / And the act / Falls the Shadow / *For thine is the Kingdom* / Between the conception / And the creation / Between the emotion and the response / Falls the Shadow / *Life is very long*"—the indecision (the principal motif already in *Prufrock*), the refusal to make the break, to abandon the "lukewarmness," stultifies existence, and "This is the way the world ends / Not with a bang but a whimper."

This is the impasse the men of the Waste Land must necessarily reach—from there they can go on only to ultimate spiritual death—or to conversion. And so the next work of Eliot is most appropriately named *Ash Wednesday,* for between it and the last poem took place the poet's conversion to Anglo-Catholicism, the most "Catholic" form of Church of England doctrine and worship, which in its "extreme" manifestations, accepts even the doctrine of Transubstantiation, devotion to Our Lady, belief in Purgatory, and many other distinctively Roman Catholic beliefs and practices. Whatever we may think of this strange imitation of Catholicism, it is a fact that it has provided Eliot with a profound understanding of the meaning of Christianity, and indeed henceforth his poetry is nourished by the most authentic sources: Scripture, Catholic prayers, and Catholic mystics, such as St. John of the Cross and Julian of Norwich. If many critics have noticed also in his later work the still powerful influence of Puritan morality, this need not be considered a defect. Neither the New Testament nor the Church and her saints have ever taught that Christianity and immorality are compatible, much less—as Graham Greene for example more than implies in *Brighton Rock*—that a horrifying murderer (Pinkie) who happens to be a Catholic by baptism, lives on a higher religious plane than an ignorant Protestant (Ida) who lives according to her own lights and believes at least in kindness and justice, if not in a very exalted virtue. No less an authority than Our Lord Himself has told us that the Samaritan, who had not the right Jewish faith but showed mercy to the man who had fallen among the robbers, was to be preferred to the priest and Levite who, though perfectly orthodox, went unfeelingly past their neighbor in distress; and He insisted times without number that an outward profession of faith is useless unless it is accompanied by a life according to the will of God, which is a life according to the commandments: "Not every one that saith to me, Lord, Lord, shall enter into the kingdom of heaven; but he that doth the will of my Father who is in heaven"

(Matth. 7:21). It is quite true that Christ came to save sinners, but He came to *save* them by freeing them from their sin and enabling them to live a life of sanctity. And this is just what Eliot shows again and again in his later works: the saving grace of Christ working very unobtrusively but very effectively in a very sinful, very miserable world.

It is first seen in its work of purification in *Ash Wednesday*, when it demands the total break—not only with the evils of *The Waste Land*, but also with natural beauty, to make the soul receptive for Christ. "Because I do not hope to turn / Desiring this man's gifts and that man's scope / I no longer strive to strive towards such things / . . . Because I know that time is always time / And place is always and only place / . . . I renounce the blessed face / . . . And pray to God to have mercy upon us / And I pray that I may forget / These matters that with myself I too much discuss / . . . Teach us to care and not to care / Teach us to sit still. Pray for us sinners now and at the hour of our death." The multiplicity of things, of thought, ambitions, desires must all be left behind, swept away on a great wave of detachment: "Teach us to care and not to care"—the man fresh from the superficial excitements of the Waste Land must learn once more "to sit still," to listen—and for that he needs help, the help of Mary, whom the poet hymns in the next section. Under the juniper tree (where Elias once sat) three white leopards have fed on the sinner's body, leaving only the bones: "And God said Shall these bones live?" as He once said to the prophet Ezechiel. By the intercession of "the Lady" who "is withdrawn / In a white gown, to contem-

plation / . . . Lady of silences / Calm and distressed / . . .
Exhausted and live-giving" the bones, which accept their
fate, for they are "glad to be scattered, we did little good
to each other" will live again, and the man who has died
the spiritual death will begin the mystical ascent, which
all the temptations of the earth "Lilac and brown hair; /
Distraction music of the flute" cannot hinder: "Strength
beyond hope and despair / Climbing the third stair." The
hatred of the empty world, so strong in the earlier poems,
is calmed, too, in the agonized question: "Will the veiled
sister pray for / Those who walk in darkness, who chose
thee and oppose thee. . . . Will the veiled sister between
the slender / Yew trees [the symbol of death] pray for
those who offend her / And are terrified and cannot surrender" . . . and in the end the prayer of final surrender
in the terms of the *Anima Christi:* "Blessed Sister, holy
mother . . . / Suffer us not to mock ourselves with false-
hood / . . . Suffer me not to be separated / And let my cry
come unto Thee."

The despairing vision of the world as the Waste Land
has given place to the vision of fallen men as redeemed
by Christ, as members of the Mystical Body sheltered by
the prayers of the Virgin and the saints. The *Four Quartets* complete Eliot's vision of the Christian life, a life in
which contemplation and action, time and eternity are
beautifully integrated. Dante had been his inspiration
from the beginning, but now St. John of the Cross, too,
the mystical doctor who was at the same time also a very
great poet, has exercised a profound influence, especially
his conception of the purification of the soul as a Dark
Night. This is already hinted in the First of the Quartets,

Burnt Norton: "... descend only / Into the world of perpetual solitude / ... Internal darkness, deprivation / And destitution of all property, / Desiccation of the world of sense"—a darkness opposed to the dim twilight of the Waste Land in which live "the time-ridden faces / Distracted from distraction by distraction / Filled with fancy and empty of meaning." For this darkness is "the darkness of God" and to arrive there "You must go by a way wherein there is no ecstasy. / In order to arrive at what you do not know / You must go by a way which is the way of ignorance. / In order to possess what you do not possess / You must go by the way of dispossession" (*East Coker*). This is the negative way of the Christian mystical tradition, the only way by which the futility of our modern world can be overcome and existence be given a meaning. But this in itself is not enough. A diseased world needs not only subjective abnegation but also objective cure, and so in the following section of *East Coker,* Eliot introduces Christ—the wounded surgeon—our Lady— the dying nurse—and the eucharistic food of "dripping blood" and "bloody flesh" and the "frigid purgatorial fires / Of which the flame is roses, and the smoke is briars" —a series of modern paradoxes to express the eternal paradoxes of the Christian life.

For Eliot is very conscious of these paradoxes, and especially of the paradoxical interplay between divine grace and human effort: "For us, there is only the trying. / The rest is not our business." (*East Coker* V), between the "mystical moment" and the everyday life of the Commandments: "For most of us, there is only the unattended / Moment, the moment in and out of time /

The distraction fit, lost in a shaft of sunlight / . . . or music heard so deeply / That it is not heard at all, but you are the music / While the music lasts. / These are only hints and guesses, / Hints followed by guesses; and the rest / Is prayer, observance, discipline, thought and action." Both, the "mystical moment" and the daily observance are united in the Incarnation: "Here the impossible union / Of spheres of existence is actual / Here the past and future / Are conquered and reconciled" (*The Dry Salvages* V), because the uncreated God has descended into the sphere of creation.

The fullness of reconciliation and union between God and man is expressed in the Fourth of the Quartets, *Little Gidding*, which takes its name from a manor in Huntingdonshire (England), where early in the seventeenth century, Nicholas Ferrar, an Anglican, lived with his family and friends a semi-religious life of prayer and work under a definite rule. All strife of earth and all earth's sufferings are, after all, transitory: "These men, and those who opposed them / And those whom they opposed / Accept the constitution of silence / And are folded in a single party" (III). ". . . And any action / Is a step to the block, to the fire, down the sea's throat / Or to an illegible stone: and that is where we start." For death is the door to the true life, when we have been purified by the fire of divine love. In this last of the Quartets, Eliot leaves St. John of the Cross for the English mystic, Mother Julian of Norwich, who is the mystic of the final harmony of all things; and whose words "Sin is behovely" and "All shall be well and all manner of things shall be well" he uses in this poem as he had used the words of St. John of the Cross in *East*

Coker. For the union of all creation with its Creator, which St. Paul expressed in his Letter to the Romans ("The creature also itself shall be delivered from the servitude of corruption, into the liberty of the glory of the children of God," 8:21), is the final goal envisaged by the mystic and echoed by the poet in the last lines of the Quartets: "And all shall be well and / All manner of thing shall be well / When the tongues of flame are infolded / Into the crowned knot of fire / And the fire and the rose are one." The flames of Purgatory merge into the fires of Pentecost, and the divine fire and the rose—the symbol of all beauty—are one, in St. Paul's words "God may be all in all" (I Cor. 15:28).

So the way of the poet, which began with the futility of Prufrock and went on to the horrors of the Waste Land, has led to the fullness of Christian hope in a new world, brought about through the Incarnation, through the divine grace that has fructified human effort. It has reached its perfection in the saint: "In a lifetime's death in love, / Ardour and selflessness and self-surrender," though it has also succeeded in the lower sphere of those "Who are only undefeated / Because we have gone on trying."

The action of grace in human life is also the principal subject of Eliot's plays, all of which belong to this later, explicitly Christian period of his life. The first of these is *Murder in the Cathedral*, the drama of the last days of St. Thomas Becket, the martyr of Canterbury. It is a medieval subject, but the treatment is modern: it is a dramatic presentation of the psychology of one who was once a man of the world, called to sanctity and martyrdom, which is traced against the background of the women of Canterbury, leading their workaday lives, fearful of the sufferings that are to come: "King rules or barons rule; / We have suffered various oppression, But mostly we are left to our own devices / . . . Now I fear disturbance of the quiet seasons." For the archbishop is defending the authority of the Church against the king and is returning to his see after a seven years' absence; trouble is imminent: "We do not wish anything to happen. / Seven years we have lived quietly, / Succeeded in avoiding notice, / Living and partly living." These women fear for their own petty security, their miserable lives, which are not fully human lives: "living and partly living." But there is something worse to be feared, which is hinted by one of the priests: "I fear for the Archbishop, I fear for the Church / . . . His pride always feeding upon his own virtues, / Pride drawing sustenance from impartiality, / Pride drawing sustenance from generosity, / Loathing power given by temporal devolution, / Wishing subjection to God alone."

This fear is not unfounded. Thomas knows what awaits him on his return to England. Four Tempters assail him, expressing the leanings of his own nature. The first is easily dealt with. He recalls his former, worldly life, "Fluting in the meadows, viols in the hall, / Laughter and apple-blossom floating on the water"—all the attractions of the senses which might still be his if he made his peace with the King and abandoned his defense of the Church. But "You talk of Seasons that are past"—these things have no longer any hold on Thomas. The next is the temptation of power, "purchased at price of a certain submission"—but to this, too, the answer can only be

"No." The third temptation is subtler: to gain his end by making common cause with the barons against the King. But this would be treachery—and to this, too, the answer must be "No." Then comes the last Tempter, the unexpected one, who offers holiness as a temptation. "But think, Thomas, think of the glory after death. / . . . Saint and Martyr rule from the tomb." And the Archbishop has to admit that he has "thought of these things." "What can compare with glory of Saints / Dwelling forever in presence of God? / Seek the way of martyrdom, make yourself the lowest / On earth, to be high in heaven." But once more it is "No! Who are you, tempting with my own desires?" Finally the Four Tempters join in a chorus that might be called the charter of modern thought: "Man's life is a cheat and a disappointment; / All things are unreal, / Unreal or disappointing / . . . man passes / From unreality to unreality. / This man is obstinate, blind, intent / On self-destruction, / Passing from deception to deception / . . . The enemy of society, enemy of himself."

"Man's life is a cheat and a disappointment"—this is the view of Heidegger and Sartre, of Camus and Anouilh; the saint is the enemy of society—this is the tenet of all the dictators of our time. Nevertheless, the saint will always triumph in the end even over his own temptations. The greatest of them was, indeed, the fourth, the temptation to become a saint for the sake of the glory it will bring: "The last temptation is the greatest treason: To do the right deed for the wrong reason." But when this has been recognized for what it is the way is clear: "A martyrdom," says Thomas Becket in his Christmas sermon, "is always the design of God, for His love of men, to warn them and to lead them, to bring them back to His ways. It is never the design of man; for the true martyr is he who has become the instrument of God, who has lost his will in the will of God, and who no longer desires anything for himself, not even the glory of being a martyr." Now Thomas is ready for his death, for "Death will come only when I am worthy, / And if I am worthy, there is no danger." And so the martyr dies, his death, far from justifying all the anxiety and dread of the women of Canterbury, has, on the contrary purified them and brought them to a deeper understanding of God's ways: "Forgive us, O Lord, we acknowledge ourselves as type of the common man / ... Who fear the blessing of God, the loneliness of the night of God, the surrender required / ... We acknowledge our trespass, our weakness, our fault; we acknowledge / That the sin of the world is upon our heads." The "common man" needs the saint to teach him the ways of God, and the sacrifice of the martyr brings blessing to the world—this is the Christian message of hope that defies the existentialist message of despair that "Man's life is a cheat and a disappointment."

In *The Cocktail Party* Eliot has given us a modern variant of the theme of hope and sacrifice. Here, too, human beings are forced to see themselves as what they are and so to open their hearts to the grace of God. The marriage of Edward and Lavinia Chamberlayne has broken down through the failure of both to see themselves as they are and so also to understand the other. They are true inhabitants of the Waste Land, living in an empty social round and deceiving themselves as much as each other. At the beginning of the play Lavinia has left her

husband, and his mistress, Celia Coplestone, is overjoyed
that now the way will soon be free for them to marry.
But Edward suddenly draws back—he, too, is one of
those who cannot make a decision—"I see that my life
was determined long ago / And that the struggle to escape from it / Is only a make-believe / . . . The self that
wills—he is a feeble creature; / He has to come to terms
in the end / With the obstinate, the tougher self; / . . . who
in some men may be the *guardian*—But in men like me,
the dull, the implacable / The indomitable spirit of mediocrity." As Edward reveals himself to Celia as he really
is, she realizes that she has only projected her own dreams
into him. They must all find themselves, their real selves,
and they are helped in this task by Sir Henry Harcourt-
Reilly, a psychiatrist who has the role of an almost super-
human spiritual guide. Through his expert treatment the
marriage of Edward and Lavinia is restored, but Celia is
shown that she is destined for a higher life—she becomes
a nursing Sister and dies a martyr's death in Africa.

Here again the everyday life of mediocre people is con-
trasted with the vocation of the saint whose sacrifice
transfigures also the mediocrity of the others: "The best
of a bad job is all any of us make of it—Except of course,
the saints." Perhaps Eliot insists too much on the gulf
between sanctity and an "ordinary" human life, for even
those who are not saints may do better than make "the
best of a bad job"; nevertheless, he is very far from holding with most of the authors treated in this book that man
is so enmeshed in his own evil that nothing can free him
from it, that even grace—as in Mauriac and Greene—
works almost wholly from outside, without producing a

true change. In what, at the time of writing, is his latest play, *The Elder Statesman*, Eliot again shows the process of purification, this time in Lord Claverton, the "elder statesman" who through his frightening selfishness has brought spiritual ruin to many including his own son who hates him. Throughout his active and partly brilliant career he has succeeded in smothering his conscience; when, broken in health, he has to retire into a sanatorium, the ghosts from the past appear to torment him: Federico Gomez, whom he ruined in his undergraduate days at Oxford and who has since made a highly successful if shady career in South America, and Mrs. Carghill, the girl whom he left and who is now a wealthy widow. Supported by his daughter and her fiancé (a couple happily and healthily in love—a welcome relief from the way love is generally treated nowadays in serious plays), Claverton at last faces the truth of his past life, of its meanness and spiritual failure, and makes his confession to them, which leaves him purified and at peace—another inhabitant of the Waste Land who has found release.

Both Claudel and Eliot, each in his own way, represent the Christian hope that neither sin nor despair are the last word, though they belong to our fallen world. "Hell is the others," said Sartre, and by shutting himself up in his own little Ego, the non-Christian existentialist closes his eyes so that he can see no way to salvation. "Hell is oneself, Hell is alone," says Edward in *The Cocktail Party*—and this realization of the true human condition as a member of a community points the way out of the Waste Land of Despair into the Promised Land of Hope.

6

MODERN GLOOM AND CHRISTIAN HOPE

IN THE PRECEDING chapters we have attempted to give a bird's eye view of what we hope to be a fairly representative selection of modern thought and literature. Except for a few "silver linings," the picture is dark, indeed. If Christianity has often seen this world as a "vale of tears," modern thinkers and novelists seem to picture it generally as a lunar landscape of unmitigated despair.

We are living in an age of wars and rumors of wars, under the threat of H-bombs, horrifying dictatorships, and general uncertainty. Yet, except for the wider technical powers for destruction, is our time so very much more insecure than other ages, do we have more reason for gloom and despair than former generations? There have always been wars, and they have by no means always been restricted only to the actual combatants—rape and arson, murder of women and children, famine and disease have always been their horrible accompaniments. Even in the Europe of the Middle Ages, so often regarded as a paradise of Christian faith and virtue, the daily life of the citizen was most insecure, the traveling merchant was always in danger of being robbed and murdered, and the absence of medical knowledge made epidemics far more dangerous and widespread than they are now: "In the midst of life we are surrounded by death," says the author of a medieval hymn. So it has always been and so it will remain to the Last Day.

It is not therefore the greater insecurity of modern life that produces the pessimistic outlook of contemporary thinkers—and we must remember that the "Father" of existentialism and all its melancholy offspring lived in the extraordinarily secure atmosphere of nineteenth century Denmark. No. Political circumstances have little to do with it, and not even personal material circumstances —for nearly all the outstanding exponents of "gloom" are highly successful authors. The spiritual situation of these writers is similar to that of the ancient pagans before their conversion to Christianity, of whom St. Paul says in his Letter to the Ephesians that they had no hope and were without God in the world (2:12). For hope is inseparable from God; if we have lost belief in God, there is nothing left to sustain us in the trials and difficulties of our life. Yet it is true that there have at all times been many unbelievers who have not held the utterly black, despairing view of life which is prevalent in our own time, and, on the other hand, some of the pessimistic authors analyzed in these pages such as Kierkegaard, Mauriac, Graham Greene, are believing Christians. There must be something that cuts across even the demarcation line that separates believers from unbelievers. Here, too, we can trace the roots of "modern" pessimism back to Kierkegaard. Kierkegaard had been disappointed in reason, which he more or less equated with the system of Hegel, and he had also been disappointed in love, in his broken engagement with Regine Olsen. Besides, his relationship with his stern, unbending father had had a very unhappy influence on his own life. That is to say the principal factors in human existence had gone wrong for him. Human Fatherhood is a reflection of the divine Fatherhood, human reason the created image of the Word of God, the Logos, Himself the image of the Father, and human love the earthly image of the Holy Spirit, the divine Person who is the bond of love between the Father and the Son. If all these become distorted in one way or another, the human mirror which was meant to reflect the divine life is broken, and what it reflects is not an image, but a caricature.

Perhaps the most serious distortion was brought about by Kierkegaard's depreciation of reason. Man is traditionally defined as the "rational animal," for his reason is the trait that distinguishes him most radically from all other living beings. True, reason can be overestimated, as was done in the so-called Enlightenment of the eighteenth century which resulted in the enthronement of the "goddess reason" in the French Revolution of 1789. In this case God will be denied, because He can never be fully comprehended by reason. But the human being will still be respected and the world will be seen as subject to man, this part of the creation account in Genesis will at least still appear to be valid. Nevertheless, rationalism carries the germ of its own destruction, because this is a fallen world; its subjection to man is no longer complete, and man himself is subject to death and suffering. This is

why existentialism is so horribly plausible to our contemporaries, especially as the fallacy of an optimistic
rationalism stands out very forcefully against a background of suffering and irrational destruction brought
about by the social and political upheavals of our time.
For, as Camus and Sartre have rightly seen, man's reason
revolts against death and suffering, and as life necessarily
ends in one, and contains a goodly amount of the other,
they feel that it is governed by absurdity—as indeed is
only to be expected if human existence is a "being
thrown" from nought into nought, as Heidegger has it.

Nevertheless, none of these authors draws from these
premises the seemingly natural conclusion that, life being as absurd and full of *Angst* as it is, the best solution
would be suicide. On the contrary, most of them preach
engagement, the deliberate resolve to give a meaning to
their life (though it has no meaning!) by helping their
fellowmen and furthering a cause, for example by em-
bracing communism like Sartre or assisting the natives
of North Africa like Camus. But if life really has no meaning, if reason has no other use than to show up its absurdity, if man is surrounded by nothingness on all sides, why
then be a pacifist or a communist, as so many "existentialists," "angry young men," and others are who imagine
that Moscow will solve the riddle of existence—why not
explode a few H-bombs to have finished with all this
absurdity and sink back into the "Nought," the *'en-soi'* or
whatever they may call it?

But man cannot deny reason with impunity. When he
drives it out by the front door, it will return by the back-
door and play havoc with his most cherished beliefs—or

unbeliefs. For the Genesis story about Adam, who was told by God to give names to the animals He had created, contains a profound truth. The earth was made for man, man can understand and use it, because he has been given reason: if he could not do so, if the world were wholly absurd and closed to all reasoning, man would long have perished, for he could never have subjected it as he has actually done. But there is, indeed, an irrational element in the world, there are powers that play havoc with man's labors, though far less so than our professional pessimists would have us believe. Christianity has never denied this—quite the contrary. The reason for this element of "absurdity," for man's very incomplete mastery of nature, for suffering and death, is Original Sin; that is, man's failure to submit to God. Man's revolt is the cause of nature's revolt and of death itself, of all the "dread" which henceforth is part and parcel of human life; precisely because man was not originally made for death and decay, but for eternal happiness.

The Christian is far from denying these negative elements in human existence; they are there, and they have their own part to play. But this does not invalidate reason nor does it permit us to consider human life and the world in which it is lived as absurd. And if the existentialists call for *engagement*, if they try to better the lot of the human race—however mistaken the means they may often adopt towards this end—does not just this make nonsense of all their basic assumptions? Sartre says "Hell is the others" (*L'enfer, c'est les autres*), and proceeds straightaway to join the communist party which has no room for the self-sufficient isolation expressed in this dictum. The old pagans, who, in St. Paul's words, knew not God and were without hope in the world, would not have dreamt of *engagement*, and devotion to the betterment of the human lot. For how can despair and the belief in total absurdity lead to such an *engagement*, except to prove that the cult of the absurd is itself absurd; that man simply cannot live without a meaning to his life? We can deny reason on paper, in "clever" books and novels and plays——we cannot deny it in our own lives. Reason belongs inescapably to our human existence.

With the depreciation of reason came the depreciation of love. Love is a much misused word, nowadays usually equated with sexual passion—in fact Graham Greene for example invariably calls the sexual act "making love." If we would bring some kind of order into the whole complex problem of "love" we must go back to the old definition, according to which it means "wishing someone well," and is primarily an act of the will; not, as is so often mistakenly believed, an emotion, though it will often express itself in an emotion. Thus Christ Himself gives as the test of a man's love for him not some fine feeling but the keeping of His commandments (John 14:15). In the same way true love of parents for their children shows itself in willing their good—which may entail sometimes an apparent evil such as punishment of a fault or refusal of a dangerous desire.

But does this conception of love still hold good in the case of man and woman? Is not there the emotional and sensual element the essential factor? This is the prevalent opinion today, and it is, incidentally, the cause of so many broken marriages. Because one thing is obvious: if love between the sexes is essentially emotional and sensual, then marriage cannot be a contract binding for life; it must be a short-term arrangement, for experience teaches that such love may cool off very quickly, and we need no Simone de Beauvoir or Françoise Sagan to tell us this. On the other hand, marriage is not, as Jansenists and other Christian rigorists imagine—and theirs is really very near to the modern view—a kind of sanctified fornication. Eve was created for Adam to be "a help like unto himself," and both were to be "two in one flesh" (Gen. 2: 18, 24); not, be it noted, two in one spirit. The sexual element is essential to marriage, for without it there could be no propagation of the race; but it is also an expression of mutual love and support, for Eve was to be a "help" to Adam, "like unto himself." The sexual union is nothing sordid, nor does it become so after the fall, else Christ Himself would not have used the imagery of wedding and bridegroom so frequently in His teaching. For the love between men and women which expresses itself most intensely in the act that is designed to lead to posterity, is also a love that wishes the other well, that is to say a love that desires the other's good (not one's own pleasure), and such a love can certainly be vowed for life, even if the intensity of the sensual passion may become less. But contemporary literature is opposed to such a view, hence it depicts the love between man and woman most often as something degrading, a violent passion that destroys both peace and dignity, and marriage as a straitjacket that must needs kill spontaneous desire.

Fortunately life is even today happier and purer than contemporary fiction; one of the most famous men of our time and he by no means a "devout Christian" could write after fifty years of married life: "My marriage was much the most fortunate and joyous event which happened to me in the whole of my life, for what can be more glorious than to be united in one's walk through life with a being incapable of an ignoble thought." These are the words of Sir Winston Churchill, and they can surely be echoed by millions of other happily married men, for whom their wives and families provided the stability needed for their work. A one-sidedly pessimistic presentation of marriage is simply a caricature, not a presentation of life as it is. Moreover, in the Christian view of it, it is not a kind of second-best for those who cannot manage the celibate life—an impression so frequently given by contemporary Catholic writers—but a vocation in its own right, in which man and woman will not only raise children for God but also help each other to approach Him more closely. In this way both mirror the divine creative activity, which was so tragically frustrated in Kierkegaard: "Marry, you will regret it; do not marry, you will also regret it"—this is the sterile indecision of the inhabitants of the "Waste Land."

A Christian, too, may want to remain unmarried—but not because he cannot bring himself, like Kierkegaard, to shoulder the responsibilities of marriage. He will sacrifice the happiness of human love for the higher happiness of total surrender to the love of God; not because human love and marriage were something despicable, but because they are the highest earthly good that can be offered to God.

For the earth has good things to give us; true, we may

all of us be called upon at one time or another to sacrifice them, and even life itself, for the greater good of doing the will of God, but this does not mean that they are bad or that we ought never to enjoy them: "The earth is the Lord's and the fulness thereof" (Ps. 23:1). And because the earth is the Lord's, earthly things can become images of the divine, signs and symbols leading us to the supernatural world. Poets are more open to this sign language of creation than other men, so it is no accident that the representatives of Christian hope in this book are two great poets of our time. But their hope is no facile optimism; Christian hope can never be that. Christians recognize the evil in the world at least as much as other men, indeed, even more so; but their ideas on evil are different from those of most of our contemporaries, including many of those who are Christian by profession, but whose views have been largely influenced by their non-Christian surroundings.

For to the Christian the greatest evil is not physical, but moral; suffering and death strike terror into the human heart, but sin has far greater terror. Our existentialist thinkers and pessimistic novelists, on the other hand, are truly mesmerized by death and suffering, whereas sin means nothing or little to them—man is always somehow innocent, his sufferings and limitations are therefore incomprehensible—and, consequently, incurable. The case of many Catholic writers—represented in this book by Mauriac and Greene—is similar, only that they are equally mesmerized by sin, and sin that is hardly curable, because it is really more a neurotic condition than moral transgression. Neither Thérèse Desqueyroux nor Félicité

Cazenave nor Pinkie or Scobie are "sinners" in the ordinary sense. They are obsessed men and women whose free will is reduced almost to vanishing point by one overpowering passion, whether this be jealousy or hate or pity. Since the prevailing philosophy tells us that reason is worthless, that man, confronted on all sides by the Nought, is in a state of dread, a plaything of the absurd, it is not surprising that Catholic writers, too, should have succumbed to this cult of unreasonableness and despair, but coloring it with the Christian concepts of sin and grace.

If this world is closed in itself, if there is nothing beyond it, if death is the end of the human being, then, indeed, our life is absurd—it matters little whether we are trying to give it some ephemeral meaning by *engagement* in a political movement, whether we commit suicide or a series of murders; there is no ultimate difference and any such concepts as moral law, justice and the rest are meaningless. If, on the other hand, man is so powerfully conditioned by his instincts that he cannot resist them and is driven into sin, even into suicide, knowing all the time that he is risking eternal damnation, then again the moral law is meaningless, because it cannot be kept.

Neither of these two black views of the world and of man is the true one. The world is not closed, it points to another world. There is a moral law, and, with the help of divine grace which works in the world through many channels, above all through the sacraments but also in other hidden ways, this moral law can be kept and man can not only be snatched to salvation at the point of

death, but can be living a fully Christian life already
here on this earth. The existentialist, and even the pessimistic Christian novelist, is cast down by affliction,
whether external or interior, and despairs—like Scobie
and the Whisky-priest. But the Christian is just *not* cast
down by affliction. Almost two thousand years before our
present neo-pagan fashion of pessimism and despair, St.
Paul elaborated a theology of hope: "We are confident
even over our afflictions, knowing well that affliction
gives rise to endurance, and endurance gives proof of our
faith, and a proved faith gives ground for hope. Nor does
this hope delude us; the love of God has been poured
out in our hearts by the Holy Spirit, whom we have received. Were that hope vain, why did Christ . . . undergo
death for us sinners, while we were still powerless to help
ourselves? . . . We have died, once for all, to sin; can we
breathe its air again? . . . In our baptism, we have been
buried with him, died like him, that so, just as Christ was
raised up by his Father's power from the dead, we, too,
might live and move in a new kind of existence. We have
to be closely fitted into the pattern of his resurrection, as
we have been into the pattern of his death; we have to be
sure of this, that our former nature has been crucified
with him, and the living power of our guilt annihilated,
so that we are the slaves of guilt no longer. . . . You must
not, then, allow sin to tyrannize over your perishable
bodies, to make you subject to its appetites. . . . And you,
thanks be to God, although you were the slaves of sin
once, accepted obedience with all your hearts, true to the
pattern of teaching to which you are now engaged. Thus
you escaped from the bondage of sin, and became the

slaves of right-doing instead. . . . At the time when you were the slaves of sin, right-doing had no claim upon you. And what harvest were you then reaping, from acts which now make you blush? Their reward is death. Now that you are free from the claims of sin, and have become God's slaves instead, you have a harvest in your sanctification, and your reward is eternal life. Sin offers death for wages; God offers us eternal life" (Rom. 5 and 6).

We have cited this passage at length, because it may well be called the charter of Christian hope, and it comes like a fresh blast of wind to disperse the fog of despair and *Angst* in which so much contemporary literature enshrouds us. St. Paul knew affliction as well as any of us— hunger, shipwreck, persecution had been his experience for years—but far from letting all this produce a state of dread in him, it gives, on the contrary, "rise to endurance." This power of endurance proves the reality of his faith, and this faith gives him grounds for hope, a hope that is not a delusion, but a fact, because Christ has died for us, and in our baptism we have died with Him to sin, we have been raised to a new "kind of existence"—an existence far removed from the existence of the existentialists, for it is an existence in which our human life has found the plenitude of its meaning. It is a supernatural and a moral existence, an existence of "right-doing," the reward of which is eternal life.

Christian hope then, while looking towards eternity, has also its powerful effects on earth, because, hoping in Christ, Christians have died to sin and must not, as St. Paul tells them, allow sin to tyrannize over their perishable bodies for they are now free from the claims of sin and able to resist it. Authors like Mauriac and Greene take the exact opposite for their subject: the tyranny of sin over the perishable body, man's incapacity of freeing himself from its bondage.

Nietzsche, the German philosopher who proclaimed that "God is dead," taunted Christians for teaching Redemption, but not looking at all as if they were redeemed. He could truthfully have said the same of our contemporary Catholic novelists: their personages profess a religion of Redemption, but their behavior completely contradicts their beliefs; they are as full of crime, gloom, and despair as the characters of their unbeliving fellow writers. But Christianity is not a religion of gloom but of joy, even in this world. The whole New Testament rings with joy: the angel of the Annunciation proclaims tidings of joy; the man who has found the treasure in the field, symbolizing the kingdom of heaven, "for the joy it gives him" sells all his possessions; after the Ascension, the disciples "went back to Jerusalem with great joy;" and St. Paul preaches joy wherever he goes: "May God, the author of our hope, fill you with all joy" (Rom. 15:13), "My joy is the joy of you all" (II Cor. 2:3), for "the fruit of the spirit is love, joy, peace" (Gal. 5:22). For the life of Christ, which all of us have to reproduce in some way in ourselves, did not end in the Crucifixion, but was consummated in the Resurrection. "We have to be closely fitted into the pattern of his resurrection" says St. Paul; the Christian life is a new life, a kind of "risen life" even in this world. For it simply is not true that such a kind of life cannot be lived here on earth, that here we are only subject to sin, to absurdity, that the death of an innocent child, like that described by Camus in *The Plague* suffices to destroy anyone's faith.

It would be folly to assert that we can understand everything in this world, that the Catholic Church has "all the answers," nicely cut and dried. There are a good many things we do not understand, and the answers we have are shrouded in mystery. We simply do not know exactly how God's omniscience and omnipotence are related to human free will (St. Augustine said we had better not pry too inquisitively into this mystery if we do not want to fall into heresy), nor do we know precisely why some seemingly innocent beings have to endure atrocious sufferings, why some promising young lives are cut short without having come to maturity and apparently useless ones survive to a very great age. We have no answer to these questions, which may well trouble a man, except God's words to Isaias: "For my thoughts are not your thoughts: nor your ways my ways, saith the Lord" (Is. 55: 8). We simply do not know the meaning of these things in the Providence of God, and the only answer we have is faith. This much we must admit. But, on the other hand, we have to affirm against our contemporary prophets of gloom that even this world is not all pain and frustration, that life holds joy as well as grief, and that it ought to be a perpetual source of amazement to them how so many people seem to be extraordinarily reluctant to leave this world when their times comes. And we have to state most emphatically that even the sufferings of this life, which so hypnotize our gloomy contemporaries, can be completely transformed by faith. It is a simple fact of experience that the fully lived Christian faith is able to overcome even the most horrifying pains, whether they be physical or spiritual. Or how else is it possible that men and women should go to torture and death singing the *Te Deum*? How else is it possible that they should joyfully bear poverty, sickness, contempt? That millions of them should voluntarily give up the comforts and pleasures that might be theirs in order to help their fellowmen? Writers like Sartre and Simone de Beauvoir are disgusted because according to them the Church teaches the poor to endure their misery for the sake of an illusory bliss in the next life—and Graham Greene justifies this view by making his whisky priest say: "Why should we make it hard for the poor man too? . . . It's better to let him die in dirt and wake in heaven. . . ." But if this were so, why did Christ exhort those who would follow Him to sell their possessions and give to the poor, why did He say: "As long as you did it to one of these my least brethren, you did it to me"? And why has it always been the practice of the saints and the religious orders to help the poor, to say nothing of the Papal encyclicals of recent times urging employers to pay their workers a just wage and to give them proper living conditions?

The hope of union with God in the next world certainly makes the inevitable evils of this world easier to bear, but it is not meant to make men indifferent to the miseries of their neighbor, quite the contrary. If the poor who have patiently borne their misfortunes for the love of God (for this is the condition, poverty in itself is no virtue at all) are promised the reward of heaven, the rich who have been deaf to their needs are threatened with severe punishment. For the Christian hope is the same for the rich and for the poor; and it works in a way that should smooth out the differences: for the rich are taught to share with the poor if they would have eternal life, and the poor are assured of this life if they accept their state with submission to the divine will.

If Christianity does not work out quite like this in practice, this is not the fault of our religion but of human sinfulness, which refuses to obey the commandments of Christ. Nevertheless, our care for the poor, for the sick and the aged, our desire for social justice and the freedom of the individual is a result of the Christian principles still alive in the West; we need only turn our eyes to the East to see what happens if men abandon hope in eternal life in order to establish beatitude on earth.

"'Our salvation is founded upon the hope of something. Hope would not be hope at all, if its object were in view; how could a man still hope for something which he sees?" (Rom. 8:24). Because the exponents of modern gloom can stare only at visible things, because the invisible is for them unreal, hope is not in them and they can only sink into despair. Even Kierkegaard could only "choose" God in a desperate "leap" into the dark, in fear and anguish, without objective certainty, since, according to him, "truth is subjectivity" and Christianity is the "absolute paradox." But Christian hope does not spring from *Angst* which is quite foreign to it, nor does it require a leap into the dark. For though its object is not "in view," it rests on a sure foundation, for it is "hope in our Lord Jesus Christ" (I Thess. 1:3) who is Himself our hope (I Tim. 1:1). It is based on the historic fact of our Redemption through Christ, who has given us access to the invisible realities of Heaven for which we now hope, but which we shall one day possess.

In the light of this hope all things fall into their place. The sufferings of this world, however severe, will not cause despair, because they must come to an end; our reason, puzzled by so much that seems "absurd" will then be enlightened, our love will be purified and perfected, and this world of ours will be seen not as a transitory stage between nought and nought, but as the way that leads to our true home.